LLC

QuickStart Guide®

LLC

QuickStart Guide®

The Simplified Beginner's Guide to
Forming a Limited Liability Company,
Understanding LLC Taxes,
and Protecting Personal Assets

Matthew C. Lewis, Esq.

Editor: Marilyn Burkley
Cover Illustration and Design: Nicole Daberkow, Copyright © 2024 by ClydeBank Media LLC
Interior Design & Illustrations: Nicole Daberkow, Katie Donnachie, Copyright © 2024 by ClydeBank Media LLC

First Edition - Last Updated: March 22, 2024

ISBN-13: 9781636101033 (paperback) | 9781636101040 (hardcover) | 9781636101064 (audiobook) | 9781636101057 (eBook) | 9781636101071 (spiral-bound)

Publisher's Cataloging-In-Publication Data
(Prepared by The Donohue Group, Inc.)

Names: Lewis, Matthew C. (Matthew Coy), author.
Title: LLC QuickStart Guide : the simplified beginner's guide to forming a limited liability company, understanding LLC taxes, and protecting personal assets / Matthew C. Lewis.
Other titles: LLC QuickStart Guide | QuickStart guides
Description: [Albany, New York] : ClydeBank Media, [2023] | Includes bibliographical references and index.
Identifiers: ISBN: 978-1-63610-103-3 (paperback) | 978-1-63610-104-0 (hardcover) | 978-1-63610-107-1 (spiral-bound) | 978-1-63610-105-7 (eBook/ePub)
Subjects: LCSH: Private companies--United States--Handbooks, manuals, etc. | Private companies--Taxation--United States--Handbooks, manuals, etc. | Private companies--United States--Management--Handbooks, manuals, etc. | Limited liability--United States--Handbooks, manuals, etc. | Entrepreneurship--United States--Handbooks, manuals, etc. | Small business--United States--Handbooks, manuals, etc. | LCGFT: Handbooks and manuals. | BISAC: BUSINESS & ECONOMICS / Entrepreneurship. | BUSINESS & ECONOMICS / Taxation / Small Business. | BUSINESS & ECONOMICS / Small Business.
Classification: LCC: KF1380 .L47 2023 | DDC: 346.730668--dc23

Library of Congress Control Number: 2023947459

Author ISNI: 0000 0005 1275 9644

Ordering Information: Please visit go.quickstartguides.com/wholesale or call (800) 340-3069. Special discounts are available on quantity purchases by corporations, associations, and others.

Copyright © 2024
www.quickstartguides.com
All Rights Reserved

ISBN-13: 978-1-63610-103-3 (paperback)
ISBN-13: 978-1-63610-107-1 (spiral bound)

OVER **1 MILLION**
READERS **LOVE**

QuickStart Guides

After reading this book, I must say that it has been one of the best decisions of my life!

— ROHIT R.

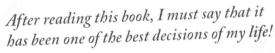

Contents

PART III – THE LIFE CYCLE OF AN LLC

BEFORE YOU START READING, DOWNLOAD YOUR FREE DIGITAL ASSETS!

 **Sample Operating Agreement**

 **State-by-State LLC Formation Guide**

 **Business Plan Template**

 **LLC Formation Checklist**

TWO WAYS TO ACCESS YOUR FREE DIGITAL ASSETS

Use the camera app on your mobile phone to scan the QR code
or visit the link below and instantly access your digital assets.

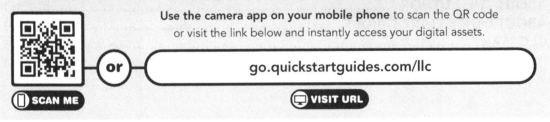

or go.quickstartguides.com/llc

SCAN ME   **VISIT URL**

Introduction

If you're thinking about starting a business or are actively planning to do so, you're in good company. More than five million businesses were started in 2022, according to data from the U.S. Census Bureau. That's the most of any year on record except for 2021, when a whopping 5.4 million new business applications were filed. The upsurge in entrepreneurship began during the pandemic, when many people lost their jobs and got creative about other ways to make some money, or just decided they'd rather be on their own instead of working for somebody else. Whether or not the trend will continue remains to be seen, but I'm encouraged by the optimism and tenacity of so many people.

I see some of these qualities firsthand, because a good part of my time is spent advising clients or potential clients who are looking to start their own businesses, and it's a part of my work that I especially enjoy. A problem for a lot of people, though, is that they don't have the financial resources to hire someone like me to guide them through a business startup, including procedures like setting up a limited liability company (or LLC for short). There have been way too many times when someone has called or come to my office looking for guidance without having considered the fee I would need to charge them. I love to help people, but I can't work for free, meaning that those calls and visits often end in disappointment.

After another batch of these phone calls recently, I got thinking about that dilemma, and decided there was something I could do about it. When you get right down to it, the steps you need to follow and paperwork you need to file in order to start a business aren't all that difficult. If you know what you need to do and where to find the information you need, getting your own LLC up and running is something that most reasonably intelligent people can do without too much trouble. I thought if I could get the basic information someone would need to start their LLC outlined in a book, it could help a lot of folks who don't have the financial resources to hire a professional to walk them through the process. That's what I've endeavored to do, and I truly hope you'll use this book to educate yourself so that you'll be able to start your own LLC.

To be clear, this isn't the only resource you'll need to open and run a business. I don't provide information about choosing a type of business that makes sense for you, or talk about market research, or take a deep dive into financials, or marketing, or any of a number of topics you'll encounter once your business is established and operating. But I believe that if you use this book as a guide to getting an LLC set up and registered to do business, you'll be able to do that successfully.

Another caveat I'll put out there is that this book is a general guide to starting an LLC and is not specific to any one state. I live and have my business—a professional LLC—registered in Texas, so that's the state and the laws I know best. The book, however, isn't about Texas LLCs. It's about LLCs in general, and the rules that most often apply to them, even though those rules vary from state to state. It's important that you get familiar with the state where your LLC will be registered and gain an understanding of what's required and how LLCs must operate. I strongly recommend that you spend some time on the website that's relevant to your state, getting familiar with the offices you'll be dealing with and up to speed on information you'll need.

I wish you all the best as you begin the journey of forming an LLC and getting your business started. I hope you'll take advantage of the digital assets that are included with this book and use the additional information contained in the appendices. I believe this book is your guide to getting you where you want to be quickly and as painlessly as possible. Let's get reading and make that happen!

How This Book is Organized

The book is divided into three parts. The first part, "Getting Started," is intended to provide the information you need in the earliest stages of figuring out your LLC. A business plan is integral to starting any type of business, so we'll spend a little time there before moving onto different kinds of business entities. I'm assuming you chose this book because you've decided to start an LLC, but you still will benefit from knowing what other entities are out there. This part of the book also takes into consideration that you might already be running a business as a sole proprietor or with a partner but have never registered the business and are now looking for the protections and options that an LLC affords.

Part II, "Getting Your LLC Up and Running," contains the nuts and bolts of the book with thorough discussions of Articles of Organization, a document that every state requires of LLCs; the all-important operating agreement that every LLC should have; how your LLC will be taxed; and whether you'll run it yourself or bring in a manager to do so. These are big topics, so be sure to spend the time you need on the four chapters within this part of the book.

The third part, "The Life Cycle of an LLC," advises on how to keep your business in compliance with your state and the importance of running your business with intention and integrity. The beauty of an LLC is the protection it offers from personal liability in the event of debt or a lawsuit, but that protection can be lost if you treat your LLC as an alter ego of yourself rather than a business. You'll find all the information you'll need regarding that scenario and how to avoid it. The last chapter in this section deals with closing down a business, which may seem counterintuitive in a book about starting an LLC. But businesses close for many reasons, some intentional and some not, and having a plan for how to do that can be beneficial.

Chapter-by-Chapter

»   PART I: Getting Started

»   Chapter 1, "Getting Your Plan in Writing," lays out the importance of having a business plan and walks you through what a plan should include. A business plan is like a GPS as you get your business up and running: It will keep you on course and help you envision where you're going. Making a business plan doesn't need to be overly complicated – a simple plan is fine, and there are a variety of tools available to help you write the plan you need. As you read in the Introduction, this book doesn't get into topics such as marketing strategies, products and/or services, or market analysis, but strategies for those areas of business should be contained within your business plan. You can think of your plan as big-picture view of your business that will guide you as you narrow your focus to more specific topics. The structure and content of your business plan might vary depending on the type of business entity you decide to start, but regardless of whether you choose to operate as an LLC, a corporation, or opt against operating through a business entity altogether, you'll need to have a business plan.

»   In Chapter 2, "Different Types of Business Entities," you'll learn the basics about LLCs, sole proprietorships, partnerships, and corporations. Many people think that a business is a business, but they vary in the way that they're formed, taxed, the legal protections they offer, and how they're run. Once you understand the differences and complexities of each type of entity, you'll feel more confident about deciding to start an LLC – a decision that I think is right for just about every entrepreneur who's looking to start a business.

» Chapter 3, "Deciding to Form an LLC," will help you understand what type of LLC will be best for your business; most people set up what I call a "standard LLC," but there are also specialty LLCs to consider. Once you've nailed down what type of LLC you want, you'll need to decide what state to register it in. You'll also learn about the steps you'll need to take to name your LLC.

» A lot of people start businesses without ever getting them registered or doing anything official about them. They simply start providing a service or selling a product on their own or with a partner. That's okay, but making your business official can provide advantages you don't get when you're operating on your own. Chapter 4, "Changing a Current Business to an LLC," explains those advantages and walks you through the process of converting your business. Changing a different business entity to an LLC isn't overly complicated, and once you do you'll be glad for the protections and flexibility it provides.

» **PART II: Getting Your LLC Up and Running**

» LLCs are regulated by the state in which they are registered, and rules vary significantly from one state to another. Every state, however, requires an LLC to file articles of organization. In Chapter 5, "Articles of Organization," you'll learn why this document is important, what information it should contain, and how to go about writing and filing your articles.

» Chapter 6, "Making the Big Decisions: Your LLC Operating Agreement" will guide you through the process of writing this essential document. Operating agreements are not legally required, but they're essential to a business and I fully recommend that you spend some time and put together a good one. Once you get this document written, it will serve as a roadmap for your business and provide a lot of guidance for how it will run.

» You've got to pay taxes, but you have a choice regarding the way you'll do so. In Chapter 7, "Deciding How Your LLC Will Be Taxed," you'll learn about different methods of taxation and get some tips to help you decide what method is best for your company. You'll also learn about filing taxes, get some tips on how to minimize what you owe, and learn why it's so important to keep your personal and business finances separate.

» In Chapter 8, "Deciding on a Management Structure," you'll read about the difference between a member-managed LLC and a manager-managed LLC, and why I believe member-managed is the right way to go for nearly every small company. You'll learn that LLCs with more than one member should consider how they can best utilize the skills and expertise of each member-manager, and why all members should fully understand the tasks they're assigned.

» **PART III: The Life Cycle of an LLC**

» There's a lot involved with getting a business up and running, but maintaining operations also requires some effort. Chapter 9, "Managing Day-to-Day Operations," deals with topics you'll need to know about how to keep your LLC in compliance, such as filing reports, keeping insurance policies up to date, paying taxes, and getting the right licenses and permits. This chapter also explains what you'll need to do if you decide you want to change the way your LLC is taxed, or you want to add new members. And in the event that you want to expand your LLC to another state, I explain how to register it as a foreign entity.

» Chapter 10, "Dissolving Your LLC," explains that businesses close all the time for a variety of reasons, and that closing a business doesn't necessarily mean you've failed. In the event that you want or need to dissolve your LLC, however, there are certain steps you must take. I walk you through that process in this chapter, as well as explain some various types of dissolutions and offer some tips on how to go about selling a business, which is different than dissolving it.

PART I

GETTING STARTED

| 1 |

Getting Your Plan in Writing

Chapter Overview
- » Why You Need a Business Plan
- » What a Plan Includes
- » Where to Find Help

So, you're ready to start a business. Maybe you've done some initial research and determined that forming a limited liability company (LLC) makes sense for you, or maybe you're still deciding what the best entity for your business might be. It could be that you're still in the planning stages of starting a business, with a vision that's just taking shape. Either way, congratulations! While starting your own business is the quintessential dream for aspiring entrepreneurs, doing so demands research, a level of confidence, patience, and perseverance – skills and traits that don't come naturally to everyone.

Every time you state what you want or believe, you're the first to hear it. It's a message to both you and others about what you think is possible. Don't put a ceiling on yourself.

– OPRAH WINFREY

Whether you're working toward setting up a shop where you can sell the hand-carved furniture you've long been making for friends and family members, turning your passion for baking into a wedding cake business, or buying that vacant building to convert into self-storage units, you'll need a plan for how you're going to do so. If you've already completed this step and you have a business plan that's ready to go, that's terrific! You can, if you wish, use this chapter as a point of comparison, to see if what you have in your business plan matches my broad overview of what many other plans contain.

If you haven't undertaken this important step yet, this chapter will help you clarify and flesh out those hopes and plans you've had racing around in your head. A carefully thought-out business plan will give you a road map as you form your LLC or another type of business, run it, and grow it over the coming years. You'll also need a business plan if you're going to be looking for investors or lenders, or if you intend to include partners in your business. So let's start by looking at what a business plan should include.

Do you plan on founding a multi-generational family business? Do you want to work in your business then sell it upon retirement? Those goals should be taken into account in the initial planning stages so you're ready when the day comes.

To watch the QuickClip, use the camera on your mobile phone to scan the QR code or visit the link below.

or www.quickclips.io/llc-1

SCAN ME   **VISIT URL**

What's in a Business Plan?

While it would be rare to find two business plans that are exactly the same, even within the same business sector or industry, most plans contain the same basic elements. These elements include an executive summary of what the business will look like, descriptions of how the business will operate, what products and/or services it will offer, financial projections, and so on. This information usually is broken up into different categories within the plan. Generally, a business plan contains the following sections:

- » Executive summary
- » Products and/or services
- » Market analysis
- » Marketing strategy
- » Financial plan
- » Budget
- » Appendices containing additional information

NOTE

This list reflects how information found in a business plan normally is broken up into different categories, such as "Executive Summary" or "Products and/or Services." Don't be confused if you look at several different business plan descriptions or templates and find that both the categories and the information contained within the categories differ. As noted, while most plans contain the same basic elements, the way they are organized and presented can vary greatly. It's more important that your plan conveys a clear, coherent, and well-organized vision than matches a particular template.

NOTE

The U.S. Small Business Administration (SBA), a federal agency dedicated to small business, discusses two types of business plans: traditional and lean. The traditional plan is detailed and comprehensive, and requires more effort and time to assemble. The lean plan, which is less commonly used, just focuses on the most important points, or key elements of a plan. It employs a high-level focus and skips much of the detail included in a traditional plan. A lean plan might be sufficient if your business is fairly simple or you're just looking to get basic ideas on paper. If you're going to be looking for lenders, investors, or partners, however, a lean plan might not contain enough information to satisfy them. Learn more about these types of plans at www.sba.gov.

DIGITAL ASSETS

A business plan template is available in your Digital Assets. To access this and the rest of your Digital Assets, visit go.quickstartguides.com/llc

Keep in mind that if you're using a template to create your business plan, you may not need to strictly adhere to it or fill out every section in it. Your plan should reflect what is unique and important about your business, so consider what needs to be included and what may not apply.

Some of these categories sound complicated and, as mentioned, they may not all apply to your business. But there are resources to help you navigate the process of figuring out what you need to include and how to compile it. The best first step to determining how the various categories apply is to take a closer look at what each section should contain.

Components of a business plan.

Executive Summary

An executive summary provides a high-level overview of the company, normally including the type of business entity, its registered name, and where it will be located. It's not a long document – usually a maximum of two pages that provides basic information about the company's leadership and employees. This is a chance to capture the reader's attention by briefly explaining your business, the problem you are solving, your target audience, and other key information. The executive summary also includes a *mission statement*, which is basically a brief explanation of the business's purpose that can address some combination of its practical goal and more idealized vision for the business. It's important that the executive summary contains specific information and is written in a way that will make the reader want to continue to read the rest of the plan.

EXAMPLE

A few classic mission statements from iconic companies include these: Coca-Cola states its purpose is "To refresh the world and inspire moments of inspiration and happiness." Apple's famous mission statement is "To challenge the status quo. To think differently." And McDonald's mission is "To be the world's best quick-service restaurant experience."

Products and/or Services

This section will state the products and/or services to be offered, and how they work. Pricing, product lifespan, and other information related to company offerings should be included, along with a brief breakdown about how and where products will be made and distributed. You'll include information about your typical customer and explain how customers will benefit from the product and/or services your company will offer.

Market Analysis

Your market analysis explains who your competitors are and what sets your product or service apart from theirs. Discuss the competition's strengths and weaknesses and explain how your company can do better. You'll want to include information about industry outlook, potential barriers to entry, regulations that could affect your business, and your target market.

Marketing Strategy

The marketing strategy outlines how you intend to reach consumers and attract and retain a loyal customer base. You might include plans for advertising and marketing campaigns and what media channels you'll use to expose your products and/or services to the audience you seek to attract.

Financial Planning

Here, you'll need to discuss financial planning and projections, including monthly or quarterly sales projections and expense and profit estimates for your first few years in business. This section is particularly important if you're looking for lenders or investors. If that's the case, the goal is to explain to them how your business plans to make enough profit to repay the loans or earn a respectable return for investors.

Budget

It can be difficult to gauge the information contained in this section, such as development and manufacturing costs, staffing expenses, marketing, and other costs related to doing business. Basically, budgeting for a new business entails making educated guesses about the company's finances. When you're just starting out and have no history of past income and expenses, you'll need to do some research to learn about typical costs within your business sector. That can help you come up with working estimates for your anticipated finances.

Additional Information

Additional information you feel is pertinent to your business can be included in an "Additional Information" section or in one or more appendices. Possible additional information could include bank statements, permits, receipts, personal and professional credit histories, resumes of key partners or employees, and so forth.

Finding Support

Writing a business plan can seem daunting, but there are resources available to help.

» The U.S. Small Business Administration (SBA) is a cabinet-level U.S. federal agency dedicated to promoting small businesses. It includes a wealth of information on a wide variety of topics, including how to write a business plan (including examples of plans), procure funding, manage finances, hire and manage employees, open business bank accounts, get business insurance, apply for licenses and permits, and many other tasks associated with starting and running a business. The SBA has district offices located across the country, which you can access by typing your zip code into a search on its website. It also sponsors Small Business Development Centers, mostly located at colleges and universities, that provide counseling and assistance for small business owners. You can learn about all SBA services at www.sba.gov.

» SCORE is a national nonprofit that helps entrepreneurs plan, launch, manage, and grow their businesses. The organization, which is a resource partner with the SBA, offers educational workshops, training, online resources, and on-demand courses. It probably is best known, however, for its free mentoring program. Entrepreneurs are paired with experienced, volunteer business mentors who meet on an ongoing basis to provide advice and guidance. You can find a mentor in your area by going to SCORE's website at www.score.org and entering your zip code.

» There are a variety of apps designed to help you create a business plan. Some recommended by the personal finance website NerdWallet include the following:

- GoSmallBiz, which, in addition to business plan software, includes software to help you navigate business and legal forms, build a website, and perform other tasks. It's available for about $40 a month, with no contracts and free cancellation.

- Enloop, an app that walks users through all the steps of writing a business plan and automatically generates sales, profits and loss, cash flow, and balance sheets based on information entered. You can get a free, seven-day plan, and paid versions ranging from about $11 to $40 a month, depending on features and whether you pay monthly or annually.

- Bizplan, which is described as the best business plan software for startups that are looking to get loans or attract investors. It includes a step-by-step business plan builder, as well as courses, masterclass videos, and how-to-guides. It also enables you to connect with Fundable, a fundraising platform that enables startups to connect with a network of backers with the goal of raising capital.

» There also are some good books to walk you through the process of creating a business plan. Some that come highly recommended include the following:

- *Hurdle. The Book on Business Planning*, by Tim Berry. Berry is a renowned expert on business planning. *Hurdle*, now in its fifth edition, provides a step-by-step guide to crafting a business plan, complete with a 53-page workbook you can use to write the plan as you read.

- *The Complete Book of Business Plans: Simple Steps to Writing Powerful Business Plans*, by Brian Hazelgren and Joseph Covello. This book includes more than a dozen business plan templates to give readers a look at different methods of writing one. It also includes some good, practical advice on starting and running a business.

- *Starting a Business QuickStart Guide*, by Ken Colwell, PhD, MBA. This comprehensive title explores the art of writing a business plan and provides valuable information about pricing, competition, marketing, identifying customers, and other components of running a business.

- *Anatomy of a Business Plan: The Step-by-Step Guide to Building a Business and Securing Your Company's Future*, by Linda Pinson. Part of the Small Business Strategies Series, this book includes step-by-step advice, five actual business plans, and blank forms and worksheets for readers to fill out as they go.

- *Writing a Convincing Business Plan*, by Arthur R. DeThomas, Stephanie Derammelaere, and Steven Fox. This book presents hard questions to get you to think about and describe your business. Part of Barron's Business Library Series, the book is methodical and no-nonsense, with readers assured that if they follow the steps it contains they'll be able to produce a professional-grade business plan.

Chapter Recap

» A business plan is an important step in clarifying start-up plans.

» Business plans vary tremendously, but most include some basic information.

» There is help available for writing your business plan.

| 2 |

Different Types of Business Entities

Chapter Overview

- » LLCs
- » Sole Proprietorships and Partnerships
- » Corporations
- » Deciding What's Best for Your Business

Because you're reading this book about Limited Liability Corporations (LLCs), I'm assuming you've given it some thought and concluded that forming an LLC makes sense for your business. And in nearly every case, I would agree with you. I think it's worthwhile, however, to spend just a little time exploring other types of business entities, just so you can understand the differences.

Something important to understand up front is that there's a distinction between the act of starting and running a business, and the act of running a business entity that's been formed at the state level by filing documents with a state agency – usually the secretary of state.

Let's take a look at a hypothetical example of the differences between the two. If Jack started earning extra cash by smoking ribs and chicken and selling the food to his neighbors when he was a teenager, and ten years later he's saved enough money to buy a food truck and sell his barbeque at outdoor festivals, street fairs, and other locations where people are looking for some food, then he's got a business going. It doesn't matter if he's officially formed and registered his business or not. Anyone who gets paid to provide goods or services to clients has a business and is responsible for reporting income and any wages paid to employees to the IRS. In Jack's case, he's operating as a *sole proprietor*, which is someone who owns and runs a business on their own. It's a very common practice, but it comes with risks.

If Jack's buddy Miguel has joined Jack and they're splitting income and expenses and running the food truck business together under their own names, they've got a *general partnership* going. As with a sole proprietorship, forming a general partnership doesn't require filing paperwork or taking any specific action at all – it's basically a default move. It's just two or more people running a business together without the benefit of a business entity. It's perfectly legal, but usually not the best way to operate.

In this QuickClip, I go into further detail about why it's so important to treat a business entity as separate from its owners.

To watch the QuickClip, use the camera on your mobile phone to scan the QR code or visit the link below.

or www.quickclips.io/llc-2

SCAN ME **VISIT URL**

To reduce personal risk and perhaps improve your tax situation, it's recommended that you take the time and effort to form a business entity, such an LLC or a corporation. Let's start by taking a look at LLCs and how they protect you and your business. Keep in mind that later in the book we'll be taking a deeper dive into topics related to LLCs that are discussed briefly in this chapter.

MY TAKE

I believe that, in most cases, an LLC is the business entity that makes the most sense for a small business. They're the most flexible, especially for a business just getting started. Starting a corporation is appropriate in some cases, but unless you're planning on taking your company public or trying to find a lot of seed funding, an LLC is probably the way to go.

LLCs

Limited liability companies, or LLCs, were first introduced in Wyoming in 1977, but the concept was slow to be accepted and adopted by other states. LLCs finally gained general acceptance during the 1990s, and now are the most common type of business entity in the United States, as you can see in Figure 2. An LLC is its own legal entity, independent of its owner or owners.

LEGAL STRUCTURES OF U.S. SMALL BUSINESSES

fig. 2

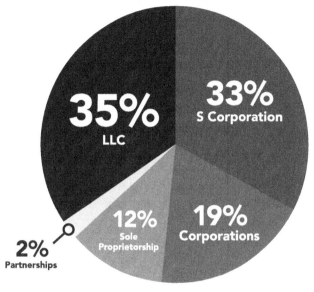

35% LLC

33% S Corporation

19% Corporations

12% Sole Proprietorship

2% Partnerships

Source: National Small Business Association

Entrepreneurs tend to like LLCs because they're relatively easy to start, and they generally don't take an inordinate amount of work to keep current. Initial fees required to start an LLC vary widely from state to state, but range from between $50 and $200 in most states.

After you're up and running, you'll encounter ongoing fees that are necessary to keep the LLC in compliance with state and federal laws. These fees also vary by state and are necessary to cover the costs such as an annual franchise tax; business license renewals; and filing annual reports, as is required in most states. You can find a list of LLC filing fees and ongoing LLC fees for every state in Appendix I. One of the most common fees is for filing your *Articles of Organization*, a public document that an LLC is required to file in the state in which it will be based. The document contains basic information relevant to your business; I go into greater detail about this aspect of your LLC in chapter 5.

In addition to fees for filing your Articles of Organization, you may encounter up-front fees for optional services such as reserving a name or applying for a fictitious business name, which is a name that's different from the registered name of the business.

So why are people willing to pay these fees, however modest they might be? The most important benefit of LLCs is that they provide protection from personal liability for business owners. The owner or owners of an LLC are called **members**, and the terms are used interchangeably. There is no limit to the number of members—or owners—that an LLC can have, and members can be individuals, other business entities, and even trusts. An LLC with one member is called a **single-member LLC**, while an LLC with two or more members is a **multi-member LLC**.

With an LLC, members are usually not personally liable for the actions of the company. This legal barrier between the members and potential creditors—sometimes referred to as a "liability shield"—protects the owner's personal assets, such as bank accounts, homes, cars, investments, and so forth, from liability and debt. If the business is sued or creditors are seeking to collect from it, only the assets of the business are in play. There are instances, however, in which an owner might be personally liable, such as if they pledged personal property as collateral on a loan that the LLC couldn't pay back. There's also a situation known as **piercing the corporate veil**, which is when a court ignores the limited liability of an LLC and holds its officers, directors, and members personally liable for its debts. You'll learn all about how that could happen in chapter 9.

This chapter gives you the essentials of what is meant by "liability shield" and how they work. For a more in-depth explanation that I offer my clients, check out my QuickClip where I get further into the nitty-gritty.

To watch the QuickClip, use the camera on your mobile phone to scan the QR code or visit the link below.

or

www.quickclips.io/llc-3

SCAN ME   **VISIT URL**

While this book is geared for people interested in forming an LLC for their small business, not all LLCs are small. ExxonMobil, Alphabet (the parent company of Google LLC), and PepsiCo Inc. all utilize

LLCs in their organizational structure. Often, however, large LLCs are subsidiaries that are owned by the main corporation. For example, ExxonMobil Sales & Supply, LLC is owned by ExxonMobil Corp.

Generally speaking, however, LLCs provide a level of protection for members, and they also allow some flexibility in the way your business is taxed. By default, LLCs are taxed as either a sole proprietorship or a partnership, depending if the LLC has one owner or more than one.

If you're the only member of an LLC, you report income and expenses on your annual taxes using Form 1040, Schedule C, just as you would as a sole proprietor, and you pay taxes to the IRS based on your personal income rate. The same normally applies to state and local income taxes. With a multi-member (more than one owner) LLC, each member pays income tax based on their percentage of ownership, similar to a partnership. Accordingly, each member claims any tax deductions or tax credits the LLC is eligible for based on their percentage of ownership. Members who work in the LLC are normally considered to be self-employed, meaning they must pay Social Security and Medicare taxes on their share of the profits.

That said, however, members of an LLC can choose not to be taxed as a sole proprietorship or a partnership. They can, instead, have the entity classified as a corporation for tax purposes. Doing so can provide tax advantages without affecting the LLC's legal status. Under this method of taxation, members are paid as company employees and participate in company benefit programs, which can result in paying less taxes. Members also avoid paying the self-employment tax, as they're considered shareholders of the corporation rather than self-employed.

A downside to being taxed as a corporation is that in some instances you may be taxed twice—on the net earnings of the corporation and on the distributions you receive. You'll need to do some research, and perhaps seek some professional advice, on whether you'd benefit from electing to have your LLC taxed like a corporation. You'll learn more about how LLCs are taxed and which form of taxation is best for your business in chapter 7.

One other benefit of an LLC is the flexibility you have in deciding how it will be managed. While the member of a single-member LLC is automatically considered to be the manager, a multi-member LLC has options. A member or members can manage the business and take responsibility for the day-to-day decisions, or they can hire a professional manager or managers to run the LLC. That manager or managers can be members of the LLC, but they do not have to be. It's my experience that most LLC members want to be their own managers, and I would personally not recommend that an LLC owner name a non-member as a legal manager of the business. Sometimes, members who are looking for someone with additional experience do hire a professional manager, but that comes with a lot of risk, which we'll discuss further in chapter 8. In a lot of states, an LLC is considered member-managed by default. To have it designated otherwise, you must clearly specify that it will be professionally managed when you file your Articles of Organization.

NOTE

An LLC can have an employee whose job title is "manager," but that's not the same as a legal management position that's filed with the state, as listed on your Articles of Organization. An employee-manager has limits on their power and can be fired at the discretion of LLC members. A legal manager, however, usually cannot be removed without the Articles of Organization being amended, and has nearly as much authority as the members of the LLC. I'd urge extreme caution if you're considering listing a non-member as manager of your LLC, as it can be easy to lose control of your organization when someone else is running it.

Sole Proprietorships and General Partnerships

As you've already read, sole proprietorships and general partnerships are default options for establishing a business. If you start and run a business under your legal name or the legal names of you and your partners, generally no further action is required; you have already formed either a sole proprietorship or a general partnership.

Still, there are instances where you'll need to file some paperwork. If you want to give your business a name other than your own, for example, you'll need to register a ***doing business as (DBA)*** name. If Jack and Miguel, who were mentioned at the beginning of this chapter, want to call their food truck business "One for the Road," they'll have to make sure that no other company is already using that name and then register it with their state.

Depending on the type of business you have, you may also need to get a business license or permit. Business licenses can be required at the local, state, and federal levels, so you'll need to do some research to know what's required of you. The most likely license you'll need is a ***local business operating license***, which is a license from your local or city government that gives you permission to operate your business. If you're operating a restaurant, gym, or other entity that could possibly affect the health of your customers, you'd need some type of health license or permit. If you have a plumbing business or operate a barber shop, you're likely to need a business license that's specific to your occupation.

If you're running your business from your home, you're likely to need a *home occupation permit*, which is a permit that lets you legally set up and run your business operations from your home. Regulations vary among municipalities, so it's a good idea to check with your city, township, or county codes to make sure you're in compliance.

Generally, however, starting and running a sole proprietorship or general partnership is pretty simple, which is one reason they're so popular. Many entrepreneurs also like the pass-through method of taxation for these types of businesses, which is more straightforward and streamlined than with some other types of entities. With this method, you simply report your income and losses on your personal tax return and pay your taxes accordingly. In a partnership, the tax you pay is based on your percentage of ownership. Income for sole proprietors and general partners usually is treated as self-employment income, meaning that, like for members of an LLC, you'll need to pay Social Security and Medicare taxes on your share of the profits.

While there are significant advantages to sole proprietorships and general partnerships, there are also some disadvantages to these types of businesses. The most significant is lack of liability protection, which can be particularly problematic with a partnership, as each partner bears unlimited personal liability for not only their own actions, but those of the other partners and employees, if applicable. Without any legal distinction between your personal and business assets, you can be held personally responsible for all debt and liability of the business. That's a huge downside to these types of business entities.

NOTE

An alternative to a general partnership is a limited partnership, which is a business entity that has at least one general partner and one limited partner and, unlike a general partnership, is registered with the state. While the general partner or partners have unlimited personal liability, the personal liability of the limited partner or partners is restricted to their investment in the company. General partners are responsible for making decisions and managing the business. The role of limited partners is to invest in the business, not to be involved in the day-to-day operations.

Another potential disadvantage of a general partnership is that every partner can enter into deals or contracts that commit every other partner. If one partner enters into a business agreement against the wishes of or without the knowledge of other partners, the agreement is still binding on all partners in the business. A bad decision by one partner can have detrimental financial and legal consequences for everyone. For that and other reasons, partners in a general partnership should definitely create a ***partnership agreement***, which is a document that outlines how the business will be run and the rights and responsibilities of each partner.

While LLCs share some of the characteristics of sole proprietorships and general partnerships, specifically relative ease of formation, a streamlined method of taxation, and flexibility with how the company is managed, LLCs have the big advantage of protecting personal assets. In my mind, that's reason enough to take the extra steps of filing documents and registering your business.

Corporations

While an LLC makes sense for most entrepreneurs, some may prefer to form a corporation because it can provide some tax advantages and other benefits. When a business is incorporated, it becomes a corporate entity that is separate from its owners. That, as with an LLC, protects personal assets and shields owners and investors from bearing responsibility for debt and liability. To incorporate a business, you must file articles of incorporation with a state agency.

A corporation is known as a ***C corporation***, or C-corp, unless it meets certain qualifications that enables the IRS to give it a special tax status. In that case, the corporation would be classified as an ***S corporation***, or S-corp. It's important to understand that an S-corp is not a business entity in its own right; it is simply a corporation with a particular tax status. The information in this chapter pertains to a C-corp that does not have S-corp tax-status qualifications. For the sake of simplicity, I'll refer to it in this book as a corporation.

A corporation must pay corporate taxes—currently a flat rate of 21 percent—on its earnings before any profits can be distributed to the business's owners, who are called shareholders. Those shareholders must then pay personal income taxes on the money they receive, as illustrated in Figure 3. This is known as ***double taxation*** and is considered a negative aspect of operating as a corporation.

The corporate tax was reduced from 35 percent to 21 percent in 2018 as a result of a tax reform bill called the *Tax Cuts and Jobs Act*. Personal income tax rates also were lowered at that time and now range from 10 percent to 37 percent, depending on income and filing status.

CORPORATE INCOME

fig. 3

SHAREHOLDERS pay taxes on *dividends*

CORPORATIONS pay taxes on *earned income*

Corporations, however, can benefit from some tax advantages that can lessen the impact of double taxation. In addition to lower corporate tax rates in place since 2018, corporations have significant write-off advantages that can reduce taxable income. They can deduct the cost of some company benefit programs, carry losses over multiple years, and take advantage of other strategies to reduce taxes. Also, corporations are not subject to self-employment taxes.

Another advantage of operating as a corporation is easy transfer of ownership. If an owner dies or decides to leave the company, their stocks can simply be sold off or transferred to someone else. Corporations also can gain access to capital by selling their stock, if applicable.

On the downside, forming a corporation is significantly more complex than starting another type of business entity, as there can be a lengthy application process and substantial fees. And running a corporation means you need to adhere to legal requirements and follow various regulations, such as having a board of directors, holding annual meetings, and creating annual reports in order to maintain corporate status.

Deciding Which Entity to Choose

Whether you're already running a business or thinking about starting one, the business structure you choose is important. Each type of structure has advantages and disadvantages, and you'll need to think carefully about which makes the most sense for your business. As a recap of the information you've read in this chapter, consider the attributes and downsides of sole proprietorships, general partnerships, LLCs and corporations as displayed in Figure 4.

GRAPHIC

fig. 4

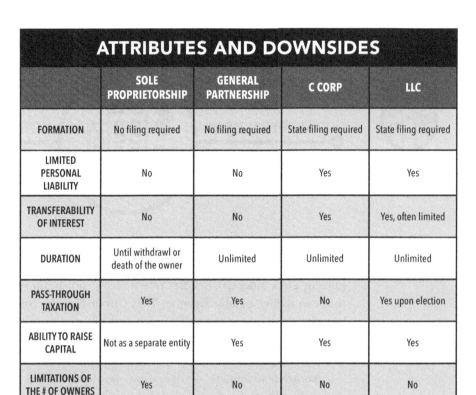

ATTRIBUTES AND DOWNSIDES

	SOLE PROPRIETORSHIP	GENERAL PARTNERSHIP	C CORP	LLC
FORMATION	No filing required	No filing required	State filing required	State filing required
LIMITED PERSONAL LIABILITY	No	No	Yes	Yes
TRANSFERABILITY OF INTEREST	No	No	Yes	Yes, often limited
DURATION	Until withdrawl or death of the owner	Unlimited	Unlimited	Unlimited
PASS-THROUGH TAXATION	Yes	Yes	No	Yes upon election
ABILITY TO RAISE CAPITAL	Not as a separate entity	Yes	Yes	Yes
LIMITATIONS OF THE # OF OWNERS	Yes	No	No	No

Use the chart in Figure 4 to compare advantages and disadvantage of sole proprietorships, general partnerships, corporations, and LLCs.

Something to remember when deciding what type of business structure you want to use is that you can always change your mind later. If you decide to start out as a sole proprietorship and in two or three years decide you need to protect your personal assets with an LLC, you're perfectly free to change your business structure. You'll learn more about converting a business to an LLC in chapter 4.

Chapter Recap

» There's a difference between a business and a business that's been formed and registered at the state level.

» LLCs are popular because they're relatively easy to form and maintain, and they provide liability protection, options for managing, and flexibility with how they are taxed.

» Sole proprietorships and general partnerships are default forms of business entities.

» While sole proprietorships and general partnerships are easy to form and run, they offer no protection from personal liability.

» Corporations, which can be taxed as either a C-corp or an S-corp, provide advantages, but are more complicated to form and maintain than some other types of business entities.

| 3 |

Deciding to Form an LLC

Chapter Overview
- » Considering Different Types of LLCs
- » Where to Register Your LLC
- » Naming Your LLC

Assuming that after reviewing the major types of business entities you've decided that an LLC is right for you, we'll move forward by having a look at some different types of this kind of business, where it makes sense for you to register your business as an LLC, and how to go about choosing a name.

As you've already read, forming an LLC is not overly complicated, but it's important to follow the necessary steps and make sure you complete all the requirements of the state in which you're forming the business. Let's start by exploring some different flavors of LLCs and whether any of them might fit your company.

The Best Type of LLC for Your Business

You've already learned the difference between a single-member and a multimember LLC, which is determined simply by whether the business has one owner or more than one owner. And in chapter 5, *"Articles of Organization,"* you'll read more about the difference between a member-managed and a manager-managed LLC, a distinction I touched on briefly in the last chapter. But technically, these are not *varieties* of LLCs; they just describe the number of members or how they're managed. Think of it in terms of cars: an eight-seat minivan is the same type of car as a six-seat minivan. But a minivan is a different *type* of car than an SUV or a station wagon.

Similarly, beyond the options for number of members and kinds of managers, there are also different types of LLCs, not all of which are available in every state. For instance, there's the anonymous LLC, sometimes known as a confidential LLC or a private LLC. This variation enables members to form the business without disclosing ownership information, but it's permitted in only a few states. There's something called a restricted LLC that requires owners to wait ten years from the time the LLC is organized until they can start taking business distributions. It too is only available in a few states, and it's unlikely that anyone reading this book is interested in waiting ten years to start getting paid, so we're not going to spend any more time on it. And there are family limited partnerships, used primarily in estate planning.

Professional LLC

- Business entity designed for licensed professionals
- Protects owners from personal liability for lawsuits and debt
- Does not shield from malpractice

Nonprofit LLC

- Normally allowable for a company owned by a single tax-exempt nonprofit organization
- Difficult to establish, as it is not encouraged as an entity type by the IRS
- Probably will become easier to establish in the future

GRAPHIC

fig. 5

Low-profit LLC

- Required to provide a product or service that benefits the public
- Relatively new entity type; not widely available
- Designed to make it easier to attract funding from private foundations

Series LLC

- Consists of parent LLC and one or more sub-LLCs
- Each sub-LLC operates as a separate business
- Popular with companies that operate multiple lines of business

There are several *types* of LLCs that I think are most likely to be of interest to someone running a small business: professional LLCs, nonprofit

LLCs, low-profit LLCs, and series LLCs (figure 5). We'll have a quick look at those, but remember that requirements regarding who can form them, where they're allowed to operate, and how they must operate vary from state to state. If you're interested in forming one of these specialty LLCs, you'll need to take some time to see if your state accommodates it, and, if it does, what is required to get it registered. You should be able to obtain this information on your state's secretary of state's website or the website of the equivalent agency for your state. You can find those websites for every state in the State-by-State LLC Formation Guide in your Digital Assets.

Professional LLC

A *professional LLC*, or PLLC, is for licensed professionals such as lawyers, doctors, accountants, engineers, veterinarians, psychologists, or architects. Some states require professionals to form these types of LLCs, while other states allow professionals to operate as a standard LLC. Like a standard LLC, PLLCs offer personal asset protection, tax flexibility, and management options. Generally, the state licensing board for your profession will have to approve your articles of organization before you submit them and other required paperwork to your state's secretary of state or other LLC filing office.

Every state except California allows professionals to form LLCs and operate under either a standard variety or a PLLC. In California, professionals are required to operate as sole proprietors, general partnerships, or professional corporations.

It's important to note that although a PLLC shields owners from personal liability for lawsuits and debts and protects them from being held personally responsible for malpractice committed by business partners, it does not prevent them from being liable for their own *malpractice* (which is a mistake or negligence that causes harm to a client, usually a patient). A doctor who commits malpractice, for instance, can be sued by a patient, putting the doctor's personal assets at risk. For that reason, members of PLLCs should also have *professional liability insurance*—better known as malpractice insurance, or errors and omissions insurance—to protect themselves.

Malpractice claims are most common in the medical field, but other professionals are not immune. Lawyers, accountants, stockbrokers, psychologists, and others can also be sued for malpractice.

Something else to note about PLLCs is that many states restrict membership to professionals in the licensed profession. For instance, if a group of engineers wanted to form a PLLC and their state allowed only licensed engineers to be members, the firm's marketing person or office manager would not be allowed to share membership. In other states, just a majority of members would need to be engineers. Similarly, PLLCs are generally restricted to only conducting business related to their underlying licensed profession. A law firm organized as a PLLC cannot also operate a restaurant; the law firm must only offer legal services and the restaurant would require its own separate business entity, which could also be an LLC.

Nonprofit LLC

The question may not be if your nonprofit can operate as an LLC, but whether it *should*. Technically, a company may be able to operate as an LLC if it is owned by a single tax-exempt nonprofit organization—think of the Boys & Girls Clubs of America or the YMCA. A regional subchapter of the Boys & Girls Clubs may be able to organize as an LLC and enjoy the tax benefits of a nonprofit because it's owned by the national Boys & Girls Clubs nonprofit. A nonprofit, by the way, is an organization that's been granted tax-exempt status by the IRS because it provides a product or service that benefits the public. Being tax-exempt means the organization has 501(c)(3) status, which it can only maintain by remaining in compliance with certain federal and state rules.

But if you do have a church or a charitable nonprofit organization and are wondering whether to register it as an LLC, I would recommend that you do not. Forming a nonprofit *corporation* is a lot less complicated and much less likely to attract the attention of the IRS, which discourages nonprofit LLCs.

This may be an evolving issue, however, because the LLC is the most common business entity in America. It seems doubtful to me that the IRS will continue to make it difficult for nonprofits to establish themselves as LLCs, but for now, I recommend avoiding it and saving yourself the hassle and risk of the IRS coming to you for back taxes three or five years down the road.

Low-profit LLC

A *low-profit LLC*, or L3C, is an organization that's structured like an LLC and is required to provide a product or service that benefits the public. It is a for-profit business and is not tax-exempt, but, unlike most for-profit businesses, which are legally required to prioritize profit-making activities over social issues in order to benefit owners and investors, making a profit must be secondary to an L3C's main objective of providing a public benefit. Some examples of L3Cs include theater groups, farmers markets, developers of affordable housing, research organizations, and motorcycle safety schools, among others.

L3Cs were first introduced in Vermont in 2008 and are still only available in about a dozen states. A primary reason the L3C was created was to offer well-meaning or socially conscious entrepreneurs a way to more easily attract funding from private foundations. These investments can be difficult for some entrepreneurs to come by because the IRS often penalizes private foundations that contribute to for-profit organizations.

Owners of L3Cs are permitted to have these private foundations as funding sources in exchange for operating as for-profits rather than tax-exempt nonprofits. Private foundations can identify causes that are important to them and support companies that work to further those causes. Their donations are not tax-deductible as they would be for a nonprofit, but along with the satisfaction of helping a good cause, there is the possibility of fiscal return as the company grows.

L3Cs are formed in the same way as standard LLCs and must be maintained according to state regulations. They're taxed and managed like a standard LLC, with the same option of being taxed as a corporation instead of an LLC. Many experts predict that more states will allow L3Cs as the number of socially motivated businesses continues to increase.

Series LLC

A *series LLC* is a type of LLC with multiple layers that provide multiple levels of liability limitation. It consists of an umbrella, or parent, LLC and one or more sub-LLCs, also known as cells or child LLCs. Each of the sub-LLCs operates as a separate business, even though they're all created and maintained by the primary entity. There can be as many sub-LLCs as desired, each of which should have its own name and bank account and maintain its own business records. Each sub-LLC can have its own members and managers.

A series LLC can file one federal tax return that covers the umbrella LLC and all the sub-LLCs, although the IRS has raised the possibility of requiring each sub-LLC in the series to be treated as a separate taxable entity. Series LLCs may be taxed differently from state to state. For instance, California requires each sub-LLC to pay a state franchise tax.

Members of series LLCs share profits and losses, but each sub-LLC is protected from legal or financial issues that may affect another sub-LLC. If one company is sued or declares bankruptcy, it does not affect the others.

Series LLCs are popular among businesses that operate multiple lines of business and want to protect each line from the others. They are frequently implemented by real estate investors looking to keep their investments separate from one another. While the number of states that allow series LLCs continues to increase, they are not permitted in all states. In 2023, the following states permitted LLCs: Alabama, Delaware, District of Columbia, Illinois, Indiana, Iowa, Kansas, Missouri, Montana, Nevada, Oklahoma, Tennessee, Texas, and Utah.

Deciding Where to Register Your LLC

Once you've decided what type of LLC is best for your business—likely a standard LLC—you'll have to determine where it makes the most sense to get it set up and registered. Regulations regarding LLCs vary greatly from state to state, and some states offer better conditions than others as far as privacy protection, legal protection, tax rates, and tax relief.

If you search online for "best states to form an LLC," the results will almost always include Delaware, Nevada, and Wyoming, three states that are generally considered to be the most business-friendly in the nation. But this doesn't necessarily mean it will be worth it for your business to register in one of those states if you don't live there.

Despite what you might hear about states like Delaware or Nevada being cheaper or more hospitable to business, most of the time the best place to form and register your LLC is in the state where you live and are likely to conduct most of your business. Forming your LLC in your home state is generally the easiest and most cost-effective way to go, particularly if you have an office or a store in your home state or if most of the money you'll earn is generated from sales or services there.

Here's why: LLCs are governed at the state level, and every state considers an LLC to be a *domestic LLC* if it was formed in that state. If it was formed in one state and members want to do business in another state (even if that's where the business is actually located), it is viewed as a *foreign LLC*. So if you live in Texas, like I do, and you form your LLC in Texas, you have a domestic LLC. But if you live and work in Texas and form your LLC in Delaware because you want to take advantage of the tax benefits Delaware offers, Texas will consider your business to be a foreign LLC, even though you live and work there.

This would mean that to legally transact business in Texas, you'd need to register your business there as a foreign LLC. That has some significant results, including these requirements:

> » You would need to pay two sets of filing fees, one in Texas and one in Delaware.
>
> » You would need to have a *registered agent*, which is a person or company designated to receive legal correspondence on behalf of your LLC, in both Texas and Delaware.
>
> » You would need to satisfy annual reporting and pay annual fees in both states.

In addition, while you'll enjoy Delaware's tax advantages on the income your LLC earns *in that state*, any money earned in Texas will be taxed under Texas laws and you'll have to pay those taxes as well. Essentially, you pay your taxes where you make your money. A lot of large corporations that don't do business in Delaware still opt to register there because they receive beneficial tax treatment and Delaware maintains a business-centric Chancery Court that allows for consistency in corporate law for any business entity formed there. But the many benefits Delaware offers to large companies are not likely to apply to you, so the better decision is probably to register in your own state.

Registering your LLC in your own state is what I would encourage almost everyone to do, but there are a few scenarios where it makes more sense to register it elsewhere:

> » If, for some reason, you live in one state but conduct all your business in another state, it could be advantageous to register in the state where you do business rather than in the state where you live.
>
> » If you don't live in the United States but you operate an LLC there, you don't have a home state in which to register your LLC, in which case you might want to choose a state with tax advantages.

» If your LLC's business is investing in real estate, it probably makes sense to register it in the state where you'll be buying and selling or renting the most property, even if those properties are in a state that's different from where you live.

» If you form one of the less common types of LLC, such as the series LLC, then you will need to register in a state that allows that type of LLC if your home state does not.

Registering as a foreign LLC in a different state can be a good thing if you're expanding your business and opening a second location or otherwise selling your goods or services in another state. Every state has a different process for registering a foreign LLC, so be sure to check the regulations before you attempt to do so.

Something else that's important to consider is the concept of "doing business" in another state. Any LLC that "does business" in another state is required to register as a foreign LLC there. But what it means to conduct business varies from state to state. Always research the laws of a state to determine whether your LLC is considered to be doing business there and will need to register as a foreign LLC. You're certainly allowed to sell your products and services to customers in other states without having to register your business as a foreign LLC, but you'd probably be considered to be conducting business in a state if you were engaged in any of the following activities:

» Operating a store, office, manufacturing facility, or distribution facility there
» Opening a bank account in the state
» Selling in the state through salespeople or distributors
» Owning business property in the state
» Holding meetings there

While registering an LLC is normally not overly complicated, determining whether you need to file a foreign qualification can be confusing. If you're not sure about your status and whether you need to register your business as a foreign LLC, I'd recommend that you check with a qualified lawyer or accountant, because you'll encounter penalties if you do business in another state but have failed to register.

As of January 1, 2024, a new federal law called the Corporate Transparency Act (CTA) is in effect. Unless the law is struck down by a federal court, all business entities formed between January 1, 2024 and December 31, 2024 will have 90 days to register with the Department of Treasury. Business entities formed before January 1, 2024 have until December 31, 2024. Business entities formed after January 1, 2025 will have 30 days. A guide to navigating this new rule can be found in your Digital Assets at go.quickstartguides.com/llc.

Choosing a Name for Your LLC

Choosing a name for your new LLC sounds like a lot of fun, and it can be. It can also be more difficult than you might think. There are legal considerations when choosing a name, and you'll need one that no other business in your state has already claimed.

Legal Requirements for Naming Your Business

You'll need to choose a name for your business before you can file with your state to form your LLC, as the name must be included with your Articles of Organization (more about those in chapter 5). Different states have different naming requirements for LLCs, so be sure you learn what your state requires. Most states require that the name of the business include an LLC designation, meaning you'll need to add some variation of "limited liability company" to whatever name you come up with. Variations might include one of these:

> » Gilmartin's Long-Distance Hauling, Limited
> » Gilmartin's Long-Distance Hauling LLC
> » Gilmartin's Long-Distance Hauling, Limited Liability Company
> » Gilmartin's Long-Distance Hauling Limited Liability Co.
> » Gilmartin's Long-Distance Hauling L.L.C.
> » Gilmartin's Long-Distance Hauling, L.C.
> » Gilmartin's Long-Distance Hauling, LC

Using the LLC designation in your name is advantageous because it gives your company credibility. That can be especially important when you're first starting out. The designation also lets people know that the company is a legal entity that you've taken the time and effort to register.

Another legal requirement is that the name of your LLC can't be the same as that of another business registered in your state. It also can't be the same as a phrase that's been trademarked. Two famous examples of trademarked phrases are American Express's "Don't leave home without it" and "Where's the beef?" trademarked by Wendy's for years.

You'll need to conduct a name search through the secretary of state's office and a trademark search through the United States Patent and Trademark Office to make sure the name you chose is not already in use or trademarked. If the name you wanted is already taken, you can change it slightly by adding your name or another distinction. Or you can start over and choose another name.

You can't include words in your business name that imply that you're part of a regulated industry, such as "bank," "credit union," or "insurance company." And you can't include words such as "township" or "federal" that suggest your business is part of a government structure. Words that a state considers inappropriate, such as swear words, also may be prohibited for use in a business name

Registering a DBA

Normally, you're required to include the LLC designation to register your company's name, but if you'd rather the LLC designation not be part of the name as you operate the business, you can file for a DBA, which as you read earlier is short for "doing business as," once your LLC is registered. A DBA is also known as a fictitious business name or a trade name.

Filing for a DBA allows you to conduct business under a company name that's different from the name under which you filed the LLC. Technically, the filing name is still the name of your company, and it's what you need to use on tax returns and other official documents. The DBA is a second name that the business can use for day-to-day operations such as advertising, opening a bank account, applying for a loan, or renting business space. It can be a variation of your registered name, such as Gilmartin's Long Distance Hauling without the LLC designation, or it can be something completely different than the registered name.

An LLC can register as many DBAs as it wishes to, which can be helpful if you have a diverse line of offerings and want to market different products and services under different names. Keep in mind, though, that unlike registering your LLC name, registering a DBA does not give you exclusive rights to the name you choose. There can be only one Gilmartin's Long-Distance Hauling LLC registered in your state, but filing it under a DBA such as Gil's Hauling Service doesn't guarantee that you'll be the only Gil around with a hauling business.

Give this some thought to avoid finding out your business is one of a half dozen named Smith's Lawn Care or Gil's Hauling Service within a twenty-mile radius. Because a DBA name is not exclusive to a state, it's possible that the name you choose might already be in use. In most cases, you'll register your DBA with the county in which your business is located. You may be required to advertise your DBA name in a local newspaper or legal publication. You'll be able to find more information about registering a DBA on the website of your local secretary of state.

Finding a Name That Works for Your Business

This can be both the fun part and the hard part of picking a name. Think about business names that stand out in your mind. They're memorable and catchy, they let you know what the business sells, and they're original and distinctive. You can see some examples in figure 6.

GRAPHIC

fig. 6

BUSINESS NAME	DESCRIPTION
APPLE	Friendly and inviting; intended to encourage everyday people to buy computers, which when the company started were considered mysterious and inaccessible.
HAAGEN-DAZS	Foreign and exotic-sounding; conveys a sense of luxury and indulgence.
REDDIT	Mimics the words "read it," which calls attention to the company's focus on providing internet content from around the world.
NIKE	Named for the Greek winged goddess of victory who was worshipped by athletes; targets athletes of every level who are striving to achieve their athletic goals.
DOVE	Evokes simplicity, elegance, and gentleness.

GAP	Easy to remember and pronounce; supposedly refers to the generation gap, to highlight the company's focus on younger customers.
PANERA	Based on the words "pan" and "era," the name focuses on the company's Latin and Spanish roots. "Pan" is Spanish for bread and "era" in Latin means time or age, depicting the company's commitment to making the best bread through the ages.
LEGO	Short and easy to remember, the name is a contraction of two Danish words, "leg godt," which translates to "play well." The brevity of the name makes it easy to position on the company's products.

The name you choose for your business should mean something to you, because you and other LLC members will be closely associated with it. Remember that it not only identifies your company but will be the basis for the brand you'll build.

Reserving Your Business Name

Once you've chosen a name and confirmed that it's available for use in your state, you're able to list it on your articles of organization and submit the form to register your LLC. If you've chosen the name but for some reason are not quite ready to register your LLC, most states will let you file a name reservation that keeps the name available to you for a specified amount of time. If you don't register your LLC within that time frame, you'll need to renew the reservation to prevent the name from being released and becoming available again in the state's records.

You'll need to pay whatever fees your state charges to reserve your name, but if you've landed on one you really like and you'll soon be ready to register your LLC, it may be well worth it.

Chapter Recap

» Although a standard LLC is appropriate for most small businesses, you should consider other types of LLCs as possible options.

» While it almost always makes sense to form and register your LLC in the state where you live, there are exceptions to that rule.

» Some states, namely Delaware, Wyoming, and Nevada, are generally considered to be business-friendly and hospitable to new companies.

» Choosing a name for your LLC can be fun and exciting, but there are legal requirements to consider.

| 4 |

Converting an Existing Business to an LLC

Chapter Overview
» Reasons to Change a Business Structure
» Potential Tax Implications
» Methods of Converting to an LLC

Remember Jack and Miguel from chapter 2? They're the guys running the food truck business that Jack got started when he was a teenager looking to earn some extra cash by cooking up barbeque for neighbors, friends, and family. Now they've been running the business together for about twelve years, operating by default as a general partnership, since they've never formed any sort of business entity.

Everything was fine until one day when Jack and a part-time employee, Chris, took the food truck to a local street fair. They were doing a brisk business selling ribs, brisket, and barbequed chicken, and everything was going just fine until festival management told them they'd have to move the truck to a different location on the property. As Chris was backing the truck out of the original spot to move it as instructed, he misjudged his position and hit the food truck parked behind him, severing some cables and cutting off electricity to the other truck, effectively putting it temporarily out of business. The owner of the other food truck was not happy, to say the least, and rightfully expected Jack and Miguel to pay not only for the repairs her truck would need, but also for lost income at this street fair and at future events she had scheduled.

Jack and Miguel contacted their insurer and, fortunately, found out they'd be covered for most of the damage. Despite worrying that the incident would cause their insurance rates to go up and inflict damage on their professional reputation, they were relieved that the accident hadn't been worse, as it could have caused greater damage or serious injury. The accident got them thinking, however, and wondering if there was a safer way for them to do business. They realized they had dodged a bullet with the minimal consequences of this accident, but they also understood they might not be as lucky the next time something went amiss.

Jack and Miguel did some research and concluded it was time for them to establish a business entity that could help protect their personal assets. They realized that having a business entity would also be useful if they wanted to raise some financing to help them expand their operations. After considering their options, they decided an LLC would best meet their needs, and they determined they would convert their general partnership to an LLC.

This chapter is designed for those currently operating a sole proprietorship or a general partnership who, like Jack and Miguel, might want to consider converting their business into an LLC. We'll review some of the reasons business owners decide to make this change, and what it entails. I'm assuming that if you're running a corporation, you probably aren't looking to convert to an LLC, although in some cases that may be appropriate.

Although the process for converting a sole proprietorship or general partnership to an LLC is a little different than starting an LLC from scratch, it's equally doable once you understand what's involved.

Reasons for Changing Your Business Structure

As you've gathered from Jack and Miguel's story, a primary reason for converting a business to an LLC is for the liability protection it brings. If the accident involving the other food truck had resulted in a lawsuit, Jack and Miguel could have faced serious financial and personal consequences. A lawsuit, or any other event that requires a large output of cash, would adversely affect a small partnership business like Jack's and Miguel's, whose personal assets, including homes, cars, and personal bank accounts, are all tied up in their business and would be at risk.

Also, if the other food truck owner had sued Jack, Miguel, and part-time employee Chris, and if Chris had been found to be negligent in causing the accident, Jack and Miguel would have been personally liable for his actions. This kind of liability goes beyond workplace accidents; if Jack went out and bought a top-of-the-line food truck for their business, running up tens of thousands of dollars in business debt without Miguel's permission, both Miguel and Jack would be personally responsible for that debt.

But the risk of personal liability isn't the only reason you might decide to convert a sole proprietorship or general partnership to an LLC. Maybe you're tired of paying the combined employee and employer amounts of Social Security and Medicare taxes. After all, 15.3 percent, what a self-employed person will pay in those taxes for 2023, represents a hefty chunk of your earnings on top of the income taxes you'll pay. Converting from a sole proprietorship or general partnership to an LLC doesn't avoid taxation, but it gives you options related to how you incur those taxes. Choosing to have the entity classified as a corporation for tax purposes can provide some tax advantages without affecting the LLC's legal status.

WHY CONVERT TO AN LLC?

GRAPHIC

fig. 7

Reduces risk of personal liability

Options for how your business will be taxed

Increases ability to raise capital

Raising capital or finding investors may be other reasons you'd consider converting your business to an LLC. Many investors will not provide backing for a business that does not operate under some sort of legal structure. And if you're a sole proprietor or general partner, you don't have shares you can sell to raise capital or attract investors. If your business is an LLC, however, you can sell ownership stakes to raise equity capital that can help you grow the business. You'll also need a business plan and a good presentation to convince prospective investors to put up some money.

Understanding Potential Tax Implications of Converting a Business

Converting a corporation to an LLC could have extensive tax implications; converting from a sole proprietorship or general partnership to an LLC is less likely to have such implications.

When converting a sole proprietorship to a single-member LLC, it should be a tax-free transfer. All you're doing in that situation is contributing the assets of your sole proprietorship to the LLC in exchange for membership. You're essentially buying ownership in the LLC with the assets from your sole proprietorship.

Converting from a general partnership to an LLC should also be a tax-free event. As with converting a sole proprietorship, you're simply handing over the assets from the general partnership to the new LLC in exchange for membership. If your ownership and business debt remain the same, nothing will change as far as the IRS is concerned.

If you're a sole proprietor looking to add one or more partners as you convert to an LLC, or if a partnership gains or loses partners during the conversion, you could face some tax implications.

Tax implications may also occur if a general partnership has incurred business debt that one partner has agreed to personally guarantee. That debt, which is called *recourse debt*, can be used as a deduction against income that partner receives from the business. However, if the partner changes the amount of debt they're willing to guarantee or writes off the debt altogether during the conversion from partnership to LLC, the IRS could consider the reduced or eliminated debt to be income for the partner and levy taxes on it. A similar situation can occur with the transfer of a sole proprietorship to an LLC, but it's much less common.

Because laws regarding business entities vary greatly from state to state, be sure to verify any state or local taxes you could encounter as you convert to an LLC. Taxes are tricky business, and not handling them correctly can seriously jeopardize your company. I'm a do-it-yourself person and in favor of DIY when it makes sense, but don't get ahead of yourself when it comes to taxes. A qualified accountant or tax expert can protect you from making a costly mistake.

Converting a Business to an LLC

There are different methods you can use to convert a business to an LLC. The conversion could entail a merger or acquisition, or you could employ something called a *statutory conversion*, which is a relatively new conversion method that involves changing the structure of your business. It's a simple way to change a business from one entity type to another, requiring only that you file a certificate of conversion along with the articles of organization when registering your LLC.

To employ a statutory conversion, your business must already be incorporated or registered as an LLC or limited partnership. If it is incorporated or already registered and your state does not allow for a statutory conversion, you will need to form a new company, transfer any assets from the old business to the new, and dissolve the former entity.

If you are converting a sole proprietorship or general partnership to an LLC, which I assume is the case for nearly everyone reading this chapter, you don't have a legal business entity to dissolve—you're converting an existing business entity from one type of business to another type. We'll discuss the steps you need to take to make that happen, and what you need to consider once your business is officially an LLC.

Converting to an LLC from a Sole Proprietorship or General Partnership

Converting from a sole proprietorship or a general partnership to an LLC involves creating and filing your articles of organization, the same as you would do if you were just starting a business. You'll read all about articles of organization in the next chapter.

You'll also need to update your registrations and accounts, and you'll want to look at any contracts you entered into as a sole proprietor or general partnership to see if you're permitted to assign the contracts to your new business entity without the consent of the other party.

Before you can file your articles of organization, you need to confirm that your business name is available, just as you would if you were starting a business from scratch. If another business that is already registered or incorporated is using the same name that you've been using, then it belongs to that other business and you'll need to come up with a new one. You can review the legal considerations of choosing a name in chapter 3. Once you've confirmed that the name is available and filed all the paperwork to form your LLC, you'll draft and execute an LLC operating agreement (which is discussed in chapter 6).

You'll probably have to change your business's *employer identification number (EIN)*, which is a nine-digit number the IRS assigns to businesses for tax filing and reporting purposes. Think of the EIN as your business entity's social security number. To get one, you need to file a Form SS-4, something you'll learn more about in chapter 7. Because your personal and LLC accounts will be separate, you'll need to open a new bank account, and, depending on industry or state laws, you may have to apply for business licenses and permits.

Your specific circumstances will determine whether you'll need to obtain a new EIN. The IRS's website provides straightforward information on its "Do You Need a New EIN?" page to help you figure out what to do.

After the Conversion

Once you've taken all the necessary steps to convert your sole proprietorship or general partnership to an LLC and your business is registered with the state, there are still a few things to consider. Any licenses, permits, registrations, or other documents related to your business will need to be changed to reflect your new business entity and name. Even if you're keeping the same name, these documents must still be changed to reflect your designation as an LLC by the addition of LLC, L.L.C., Limited Liability Co., or another variation of "limited liability company" to the name.

Another important task is getting a separate business bank account set up. This helps prove, in the event of a lawsuit or large liability, that you and your business are separate financial entities. You'll learn more about this in chapter 7, which deals with how your LLC will be taxed.

At this point you'll establish a complete operating agreement, detailing how your business will be structured, owned, managed, and operated. We'll get into the nuts and bolts of operating agreements in chapter 6.

As mentioned, you'll need to transfer any assets from your previous business to the LLC. It should be a straightforward process when converting from a sole proprietorship or general partnership; you'll simply invest those assets in the new LLC in exchange for shares of ownership.

Any contracts you signed as a sole proprietor or general partner will need to be reviewed and addressed when converting your business to an LLC. Most contracts have a clause called "assignments." An *assignment of contract* states that one party is allowed to transfer the rights, responsibilities, and benefits of a contract to another party. If a contract you've signed permits you to assign it to another party, you can assign your duties under the old contract to your LLC without having to get permission from the other party.

If the contract doesn't permit assignments without permission, you'll need to confer with the other party about amending the contract or drawing up a new one. If for some reason the other party doesn't agree to amending the contract or giving you a new one, you'll continue to be personally responsible for your obligations as stated.

Converting to an LLC from a sole proprietorship or general partnership follows many of the same steps as forming an LLC from scratch. This chapter provides an overview of the formation process, but part II of this book, "Getting Your LLC Up and Running," goes into a lot more detail.

Chapter Recap

» There are a number of reasons to convert your business to an LLC; it is primarily done to shield personal assets from liability.

» There could be tax implications when converting your business to an LLC, so make sure you understand the pertinent laws.

» The actions taken to convert a sole proprietorship or general partnership to an LLC are similar to those taken when starting an LLC from scratch.

» It's important to check any contracts you've entered into personally, as they may have to be reassigned to your new LLC.

PART II

GETTING YOUR LLC UP AND RUNNING

| 5 |

Articles of Organization

Chapter Overview
» The Importance of the Articles of Organization
» What the Articles of Organization Include
» Filing with the State

Completing and filing *articles of organization* is an important part of forming an LLC. The articles of organization is a public document that an LLC is required to file in the state in which it will be based. It contains basic information relevant to the business. Remember that many counties and cities have business licensing and zoning requirements that need to be addressed in addition to the filing of the articles of organization document.

The information you're required to submit varies from state to state, but nearly every state has a downloadable form, which makes the process fairly simple. In addition to satisfying state requirements, your articles of organization establish and state the responsibilities of each member of the LLC.

As with many aspects of forming and operating an LLC, state laws vary. When filing your articles of organization, it's important to review specific state-based requirements, which should all be available on the website of that state's business registration authority. That authority is usually the secretary of state's Office, but not always. In Utah, for instance, the authority is the Utah Division of Corporations. In Arizona, LLC formation is handled by the Arizona Corporation Commission. And in Virginia, the State Corporation Commission serves as the authority. Appendix I contains a list of the authorities that oversee LLCs in every state.

You also can download free templates for creating your articles of organization from online sources such as LawDepot. Some sites, such as LegalZoom and Rocket Lawyer, offer services to help with forming an LLC. A free basic package might include a template for the articles of organization, a checklist of what you should do once your LLC is registered, a name check to make sure your chosen name is available, and a customizable website template. Upgraded services, including help with obtaining an employer identification number (EIN), an operating agreement template, and consultations with attorneys are available for a fee ranging from about $250 to $300.

These types of services can have value for a do-it-yourself entrepreneur who is setting up an LLC on their own. Nevertheless, I recommend proceeding with caution. Specifically, read the information carefully and make sure what you choose will meet your needs. Some paid services, for instance, offer attorney consultations about legal topics related to your business for a limited time, say fifteen or thirty days. That sounds like valuable assistance, but what will you do if you have legal questions a couple of months after you've filed your LLC?

Make sure to consult customer reviews and ask whether the company is qualified to advise on forming an LLC in every state—or at least in the state in which you're forming—as laws and regulations can vary significantly from state to state.

In this chapter we'll look at what information is generally included in the articles of organization and why creating and filing this document is an important step when you're launching your LLC, whether you're doing so on your own or with other LLC members.

A Birth Certificate for Your Business

When you complete and file articles of organization, you're declaring your intent to form an LLC and operate your business as a legal entity. Some people compare the articles to a birth certificate for your business. As you know, it's entirely possible to conduct business without the benefit of an LLC, but you won't benefit from the advantages provided by a legal entity.

One of the quirks of our two-layer federalist legal system is that states can have different names for the exact same thing. The document you use to file your LLC with the state is referred to as "articles of organization" in most states, but not all. My state, Texas, requires you to file a "certificate of formation," and in other states the document is called the "articles of formation." These are all terms for the same thing: the initial paperwork required to form your LLC pursuant to a state's statute authorizing LLCs to be formed.

Your articles of organization are a legal document necessary to operate as a legal entity. This document also function as an application, of sorts, that requires state approval before you can move forward. Although it does provide some information about your LLC's management structure, it is not a guide to how your business will operate from day to day. That information will be found in your LLC's operating agreement (which you'll read more about in chapter 6). Your articles of organization also do not provide the following:

- » Long-term business plans
- » Information regarding products and services
- » Financial information
- » A budget
- » Marketing plans
- » Other important information related to current and future plans

The previously listed types of information are spelled out in your business plan, which will continue to serve as your road map as your business moves forward.

With these limits established, let's take a closer look at what your articles of organization will include.

What Articles of Organization Should Include

It depends on what state you're filing in, but generally, your articles of organization will include the information listed in figure 8.

Name of the LLC

I covered the process of choosing a name for your LLC in chapter 3, so you can review that information if you need to. Be sure to do a search of business names already registered in your state to avoid choosing a name that's already taken.

Purpose of the LLC

Some, though not all, states require specific information regarding the purpose of your LLC, often referred to as a *statement of purpose*. Many states are satisfied with a general statement, such as "any and all business purposes for which an LLC may be organized." An exception to this is if you're starting a professional limited liability company, or PLLC, in which case you'll probably need to supply specific information about the type of professional services the LLC will provide. When in doubt, it is better to be as broad as possible, or you may risk limiting what your business can do. For example, a client of mine opened a tattoo studio. When she initially formed her LLC (without my help), she limited the purpose of the LLC to tattoo work. Before she could expand her business offerings to include body piercing, we had to amend her certificate of formation or risk losing her liability shield through the LLC.

The LLC's Registered Agent

A registered agent is a person or company designated to receive legal correspondence on behalf of your LLC. That might be communications from the state, such as business renewal notices, or any documents related to lawsuits.

A registered agent can be an individual or a business but must be located in the state in which you're registering your LLC. If your LLC is registered in more than one state, you'll need an agent in each of those states. The name of your registered agent and a street address (as opposed to a post office box) must be included with your articles of organization.

It is common for an LLC, especially a small one, to designate one of its members as the registered agent and use the location of the business as the address. If you're a single-member LLC, you can appoint yourself. Some LLCs select a lawyer, relative, or friend to serve as the registered agent, which is okay as long as the person is agreeable to serving and you know them to be trustworthy and available as needed. A registered agent must be available to accept business correspondence during business hours throughout the year, so someone who spends part of the year in another state would not be an appropriate choice, as registered agents can serve only in states in which they are legal residents.

If you appoint yourself or a relative or friend to serve as your registered agent, be aware of the potential downsides of using your home address as the point of contact. Doing so puts your home address on public record, meaning anyone who wants to contact your business can find out where you live, and that information can be collected and sold. As you may know, consumer data is valuable to businesses for marketing purposes, and there are plenty of data brokers out there who are happy to gather your information to sell to these businesses. Public records provide a prime opportunity for brokers to do just that.

Some LLCs hire a private registered agent service company to serve instead of an individual. These companies, which generally charge between $100 and $300 a year for their services, receive all business correspondence and make sure it's forwarded to you, often electronically. A national service company with offices in every state is often a good choice for LLCs that are registered in more than one state.

Explanation of Management Structure

Most states require that you indicate whether your LLC will be run by all the members collectively, (which would make it a member-managed entity), by only some of the members, or by a professional manager. If you don't include this information, the state may assume by default that the business is member-managed. If you're a single-member LLC, you are automatically considered the manager unless you say otherwise. Some states require that you provide names and addresses of the managers, while others simply require clarification of the type of management your LLC will have. You'll read much more about LLC management in chapter 8, "Deciding on a Management Structure."

Mailing Address

This is simply the physical address of the LLC. Check your state website to see what's required; some states allow you to give a post office box as an address, and others—like my home state of Texas—require a physical location. As mentioned before, documents related to forming a business entity are public records. If your state requires a physical address for your business and you intend to work from home, you will be required to list your home address.

Duration of Operations

Some states require that you indicate how long your LLC will operate. This might seem odd, as you may not have even considered how long you intend to keep the business running. If your state does ask for this information, you can probably respond "perpetual," which avoids having to be specific about the length of time you plan to operate. Some states, however, limit the amount of time an LLC can operate, requiring renewal when the term of operation ends. In these states, even if you are forming your LLC for a specific short-term purpose—such as filming a documentary or flipping a house—it is still better to list the duration as "perpetual" if possible, to avoid any conflicts if your project runs longer than anticipated.

Signatures

You'll need to include the signature of at least one organizer of the LLC in your articles of organization. An organizer is someone who gets the business set up with the secretary of state (or equivalent) in the state where the business is being organized. Most of the time, a member or members of the LLC will handle that job, but in my work as an attorney, I am often hired to do that work for LLC members. If I do the work, I am listed on the articles of organization as an organizer, but not as a member. If your LLC is member-managed, it's a good idea to have all members sign, to show that they intend to participate in the business.

ELEMENTS USUALLY INCLUDED IN ARTICLES OF ORGANIZATION

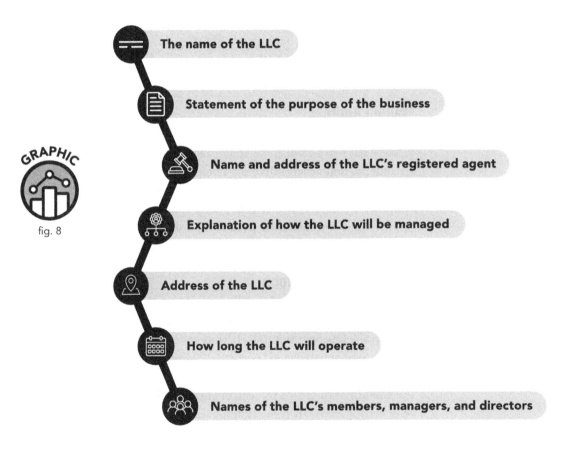

GRAPHIC

fig. 8

- The name of the LLC
- Statement of the purpose of the business
- Name and address of the LLC's registered agent
- Explanation of how the LLC will be managed
- Address of the LLC
- How long the LLC will operate
- Names of the LLC's members, managers, and directors

How to File Your Articles of Organization

Once you've completed the articles of organization document, file it with the state in which your LLC will operate. You can find instructions for how to do that on the secretary of state website. Most states, but not all, allow you to file the form online. There is a filing fee, which typically ranges from $50 to $200. Make sure to review the entire document before you submit it, making sure the information is correct and the form is signed.

A few states require LLCs to publish a notice of formation in a local newspaper or business journal. If that's a requirement in your state, you'll need to include your LLC's name, the county and address at which it's located, the purpose of the business, the name of the registered agent, and the date when the state approved the formation.

After submitting your articles of organization, your application will be either approved or rejected. If it's approved, you'll receive a document from the state called a certificate of formation, usually within seven to ten business days, depending on volume and how the approvals are processed. If the state rejects your filing, don't panic. When this happens, it's almost always because some information you submitted was incorrect or missing, the forms weren't signed properly, or there was a clerical error. You can contact the secretary of state's office to clarify the issue and correct the problem. Once any errors have been corrected and you receive your certificate of formation, your LLC is approved to do business in the state.

Chapter Recap

» Articles of organization must be filed for an LLC to be recognized by the state as a legal business entity.

» The articles of organization should include the LLC's name, its purpose, its registered agent, how it will be managed, its mailing address, the intended duration of operation, and signatures of the members.

» Articles of organization must be filed with the state in which the LLC will operate.

| 6 |

Making the Big Decisions

Your LLC Operating Agreement

Chapter Overview

»   Why an Operating Agreement Matters
»   Single-Member LLCs Need One Too
»   What the Agreement Should Include
»   Keeping It Up to Date

Starting a business of any kind is usually a stressful undertaking, so it's understandable if you're starting to feel a little overwhelmed at this point. LLCs offer so much freedom and flexibility that considering all the customization options can be exhausting. You may be tired of researching and planning and filling out forms, and just want to get on with running your business and earning some money.

While I completely understand those sentiments, there's one important task that must be completed. Whether your LLC is single-member or multimember, it needs an *operating agreement*. An operating agreement is a document that spells out the terms of your LLC based on the wishes and needs of its members. It details how things are to be done and puts everybody in accord regarding how the business will be run.

Is an operating agreement required by law? No, not in most states. But do you need one? I would firmly argue that you do. For one thing, having an operating agreement is a huge asset if you're facing a lawsuit or a large liability, which is one of the reasons to form an LLC in the first place. An operating agreement demonstrates that your LLC is a separate entity that follows a set of rules and procedures as spelled out in the agreement. It reinforces your limited liability status and helps protect your personal assets from your business assets.

I recommend an operating agreement even for single-member LLCs. In this QuickClip, I go over *why* it's advantageous to have an operating agreement even if there's no one else involved in your LLC.

To watch the QuickClip, use the camera on your mobile phone to scan the QR code or visit the link below.

or

www.quickclips.io/llc-4

SCAN ME   **VISIT URL**

OPERATING AGREEMENT

GRAPHIC

fig. 9

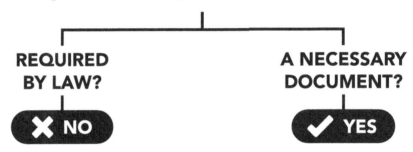

REQUIRED BY LAW?

✖ NO

A NECESSARY DOCUMENT?

✔ YES

So that's an important reason for putting an operating agreement in place—but not the only one. In addition, the agreement establishes a road map for the business and gives you a framework for addressing any issues that arise along the way. It also serves as a contract between LLC members. While articles of organization are necessary for establishing your LLC as a legal business entity, an operating agreement is necessary for setting up your LLC to be as successful as possible.

The Importance of an Operating Agreement

Let's explore the importance of operating agreements a bit further. One vital thing to understand is that operating agreements don't just apply to LLCs that generate earnings of a certain amount or have more than a dozen partners. Every LLC, even a single-member LLC, should have an operating agreement.

Many business owners believe that simply establishing a legal entity like an LLC or a corporation provides all the legal protection they need. And although limited liability for members and shareholders is generally a well-established principle, there are exceptions to the rule.

It sometimes happens that a creditor will sue the members or shareholders, asking the judge to "pierce the veil" and hold the members or shareholders personally liable. This is most common with LLCs or corporations that have just one or a few owners and are running up against major debt or a lawsuit. You'll learn a lot more in chapter 9 about this concept of piercing the veil and how to protect your LLC from it. But a good defense against it is to have an effective operating agreement in place, even if you're a single-member LLC.

Don't confuse an LLC operating agreement with a business plan. Both are important, but one is not a substitute for the other. A business plan spells out your LLC's goals and provides benchmarks to determine whether those goals are being met. An operating agreement defines the business's terms, based on the needs and wishes of its members. Those terms include things like how you choose which method of taxation will apply to your LLC or how much capital each member will contribute.

Another reason an operating agreement is important is that its rules can often supersede those established by the state. That's right: if your LLC doesn't have an operating agreement, state rules will apply by default. But states' LLC acts are typically general and vague, and won't necessarily work in the best interests of your business. For instance, if your LLC doesn't have an operating agreement, your state could require that all profits generated be shared equally among members, with no regard for how much capital each person contributed.

Your operating agreement spells out the path your business will follow, putting you and other members—not the state—in charge of your rules.

Another important function of an operating agreement is to solidify verbal agreements, which helps to avoid miscommunications and misunderstandings. Have you ever talked to a friend or partner about something, only to find out later you had very different understandings of what was discussed? That also happens in business and can result in some pretty negative outcomes. It's best to have business terms in writing, with everyone on board and in agreement.

In addition, by establishing rules for succession, an operating agreement helps protect your LLC from negative fallout caused by an unanticipated event, like the death of a member. It also outlines rules for governance procedures such as voting, scheduling, and holding meetings.

Only a few states (including California and New York) require every LLC to have an operating agreement. But I believe you'd be remiss if you didn't take the time to generate a sound operating agreement to guide you and other members of your LLC. You can draft one on your own or look for outside assistance.

There are companies that will help you create an operating agreement and review it for you, for a fee. You may want to hire someone to help you with your operating agreement, but you don't necessarily have to. In the Digital Assets for this book, we've included a sample operating agreement that you can use in conjunction with this chapter to create your own if you're so inclined. You can find this and all your Digital Assets for this book at go.quickstartguides.com/llc.

Once your agreement is written and signed by every member of the LLC, copies should be distributed to each member, and the LLC should keep a copy with its corporate records. If additional members join the LLC, they should each receive and sign a copy of the agreement. Unlike articles of organization, operating agreements are private documents that do not need to be filed with the state.

Why a Single-Member LLC Should Have an Operating Agreement

Single-member LLCs should have operating agreements for the same reasons as multimember LLCs do. One of the most compelling reasons is to protect its business liability status. By default, the IRS considers a single-member LLC to be a *disregarded entity*, which is a single-owner business entity that the IRS disregards for purposes of federal income tax. This designation is based on the fact that income from the LLC goes to only one person—the single member. The owner of the LLC pays the business's portion of taxes along with their personal taxes instead of filing a separate tax return for the LLC.

That lack of distinction between business and personal taxes can cause confusion about which assets are business assets and which are personal assets. An operating agreement can spell out which assets are which and help protect your personal ones from your business assets in the event of a lawsuit or debt. It signals a deliberate separation of personal and business operations, which is important in protecting you from business liability. It can also make it easier to identify and claim deductions on your tax return.

Just as a note, a single-member LLC can opt to be taxed as a corporation. As you'll learn in chapter 7, this comes with its own set of advantages and disadvantages.

An operating agreement empowers a single-member LLC with its own set of rules that supersede the state's default rules (as with a multimember LLC). It may also be beneficial if you're looking for financial lenders, because the agreement provides a clear explanation of how your business is organized and run.

The operating agreement for a single-member LLC should specify what will occur if the owner dies or becomes incapacitated. That's particularly important if it's run by a manager instead of the owner. If an owner dies without specifying what is to happen to the business, it's likely, although not inevitable, that the LLC will be dissolved.

These are all important reasons for a single-member LLC to have an operating agreement, but an advantage that can't be overstated is that the agreement declares your intentions related to how the LLC should be run. This can help your business stay on track and grow.

What to Include in Your Operating Agreement

There probably aren't quite as many versions of LLC operating agreements as there are LLCs, but it might be close. One of the advantages of an operating agreement is that it can be tweaked and customized to fit your particular LLC—there is no "one size fits all" agreement.

Still, nearly all agreements contain certain basic information, such as that which identifies the business, the purpose of the business, how it will be taxed, and so forth. An operating agreement is made up of various sections, here referred to as *provisions*. The agreement I use when working with clients contains seven sets of provisions, each containing a specific type of information. It also includes spaces for signatures. We'll examine each set of provisions in the next sections.

The information in this chapter corresponds to the operating agreement included in your Digital Assets. This is the operating agreement I give to clients who hire me to guide them through the process of setting up an LLC. Using it will save you time and money, and you can rest assured it's a tried-and-true agreement that's been used by many aspiring entrepreneurs.

Please note, however, that this is *your* business. The operating agreement template I've shared is just that: a template. If you want to add, remove, or edit anything in it, you should do so, provided you understand the effect that your changes will have. You are building the foundation of your business, and your operating agreement should reflect your priorities, goals, and needs.

The following sections discuss the various provisions in the operating agreement I am providing as a Digital Asset. The goal is for you to understand *why* each provision is included so you can make changes accordingly. If you choose to look online for a different template, the explanations here will also apply to most of the terms in those templates. The downside to looking elsewhere is that another template may omit important terms that someone without a law degree would not notice are missing. Tread carefully.

First Set of Provisions: Preliminary Provisions of an LLC Operating Agreement

Let's start by looking at the preliminary, sometimes called the basic, provisions of the LLC operating agreement. Much of this information will look familiar, because the preliminary provisions of an operating agreement have some overlap with the information in your articles of organization. Note that the titles of provisions vary from agreement to agreement. The titles here are those in the operating agreement I use. The same information could be included in another agreement in a section that's called something different.

» **Effective Date**: This is simply the date on which the operating agreement is adopted by the members of the LLC. The formal name of the company is included.

» **Formation**: Sometimes called a "statement of intent," this provision states that the LLC was formed in accordance with laws governing LLCs in the state in which the LLC is located, and that articles of organization, a certificate of formation, or a similar document was filed with the state. It includes the date on which that document was filed.

» **Name**: Here the formal name of the LLC is given, as written in the "Effective Date" provision. Note that the LLC may do business under a different name in accordance with the state's regulations pertaining to fictitious or assumed business names. This covers the LLC in the event that the name becomes an issue.

» **Registered Office and Agent**: Include the name and address of your registered agent. As discussed in chapter 5, this is the person who will receive official documents on behalf of the LLC. It is not necessary to amend your operating agreement if your registered agent changes.

» **Business Purposes**: Just as you did in your articles of organization, include a statement explaining the purpose of your LLC. Unless it's a professional LLC and you'll be providing specific professional services, you can keep this information vague, stating the purpose as something like "to engage in any and all business purposes as may be legally carried out by an LLC in the state of Texas" (or whatever state you're registered with).

» **Duration of the LLC**: As you did in your articles of organization, indicate the duration of your LLC's operations. Unless you started the LLC for a specific purpose with a specific time frame in mind, you probably have no idea how long it will operate. In that case, simply say something like "the LLC will continue until it is terminated as provided for in the articles of organization or dissolved under state law." If you've started an LLC for a specific purpose, such as flipping a house, you might specify a certain length of time for which the business will exist, either by stating a specific dissolution date or citing an event—in this case, settling on the sale of the house—that will cause the LLC to dissolve. When in doubt, err on the side of vagueness. You do not want your LLC to be dissolved before you are ready.

Second Set of Provisions: Membership Provisions of an LLC Operating Agreement

The next set of provisions is called Membership Provisions and includes information about members, compensation, and how the LLC will be managed.

» **Non-Liability of Members**: This provision states that no member of the LLC will be held personally liable for expenses, debts, obligations, or liabilities of the business or for claims made against it.

» **Reimbursement for Organizational Costs**: This provision states that the LLC will reimburse members for organizational expenses they incur, with an option for members to elect to receive reimbursements over a period of time as permitted by the IRS.

» **Management**: There are three options for how an LLC is managed. In one option, all the members serve as managers, handling the day-to-day operations of the business in a prescribed manner. In the second option, one or more members, but not all, are designated to serve as managers. The third option is to hire a nonmember to manage the business. The first option means your LLC is "member-managed." The second and third options mean your LLC is "manager-managed." You'll read more about managing an LLC in chapter 8.

» **Members' Percentage Interests**: Each member owns a percentage of the LLC based on how much money they contribute. If an LLC had a starting fund of $50,000, of which Renee contributed $12,500, Renee has a 25 percent interest in the business. The operating agreement would list her total contribution and the ownership interest she has. You can also elect to have all members be equal owners regardless of their capital contributions. The choice is yours. The template provided allocates ownership based on contributed capital.

» **Membership Voting**: Members normally vote in proportion to their percentage interest in the LLC. The operating agreement I use states that no action can be taken on a vote that results in a tie. Therefore, it must be stipulated whether veto power will be given to one member or a group of members in the event of a tie, or else another method of breaking a tie must be designated, such as flipping a coin or engaging a neutral third party to resolve the issue. Almost every client I work with has a different view on how to fairly resolve a tied vote, so think carefully about what you want to do in this case.

» **Compensation**: This provision is important because there could be tax consequences if members are paid directly for performing management duties. You should state that members are not paid as members of the LLC for performing management duties, but instead are paid a salary as W-2 employees, meaning that taxes on the employees' payments are withheld throughout the year. The important distinction between "employee" and "member" is that an employee is paid a set wage on a regular basis, regardless of whether the LLC generates a profit. A member, on the other hand, is an owner who receives money from profits. That money is considered dividends, not wages.

» **Members' Meetings**: It's important to include information about meetings of members in your operating agreement. If you don't, you could be regulated by state law, which could mandate a requirement for the LLC to meet quarterly, for example, or risk losing its liability protection. This provision should stipulate which member(s) may call a meeting and the procedure for doing so, and how members should respond to a call for a meeting. It stipulates what happens if some members are not able to attend a meeting, covers the issues of postponed meetings, and lays out how minutes are to be taken and stored.

» **Membership Certificates**: Membership certificates are issued to confirm that someone is, indeed, a member of the LLC. Your operating agreement must state that membership certificates will be issued to all members.

» **Other Business by Members**: This provision states that all members must agree to forgo investing, working for, or managing a business other than the LLC if those activities would compete with the mission, productivity, or profitability of the LLC. This is often referred to as a "duty of loyalty" to the LLC.

Third Set of Provisions: Tax and Financial Provisions of an LLC Operating Agreement

The third set of provisions deals with taxes and financial matters. You'll read more about these provisions in chapter 7.

» **Tax Classification of LLC**: This provision states how your LLC will be taxed. You can change the manner in which you'll be taxed at a later time, as long as all members agree.

» **Tax Year and Accounting Method**: This provision states whether you'll use the cash method of accounting or the accrual method. Most small businesses choose cash accounting: you're taxed on money based on when you receive it, rather than on when the work for which payment is due was completed.

» **Tax Matters Partner**: Your LLC could be required under Internal Revenue Code regulations to have a designated *tax matters partner*, which is someone within the LLC who serves as its spokesperson in any dealings with the IRS. The designated partner is responsible for communicating their interactions with the IRS to other members of the LLC.

» **Annual Income Tax Returns and Reports**: This states that each member of the LLC must be provided with copies of the LLC's state and federal income tax returns within sixty days after the end of the tax year. Members also must be provided with any information and forms necessary for them to complete their individual tax returns.

» **Bank Accounts**: This provision states which banks the LLC will work with and which members are designated to deposit and withdraw LLC funds. It also stipulates that LLC funds should not be commingled with the personal funds of any LLC member.

» **Title to Assets**: The LLC will likely have some kind of assets or property, and this provision states that all the LLC's property is held in the name of the LLC, rather than in the names of individual members.

Fourth Set of Provisions: Capital Provisions of an LLC Operating Agreement

The fourth set of provisions deals with how capital contributions are handled. These provisions are important because failing to contribute an appropriate amount of capital to the LLC can play a role in whether legal representatives or entities can pierce your LLC's liability shield in the event of a lawsuit. In this context, "capital" refers to money or services being invested in the business. You are building an asset, and this section revolves around your investment in that asset.

» **Capital Contributions by Members**: This states the amount of cash, property, and/or services that each member contributes to the LLC. It also indicates the percentage interest that each member receives in return for their capital contribution. As mentioned in the second set of provisions, you can elect to make all members equal owners regardless of their capital contributions. Even if you do this, however, you should still list their contributions. And don't shortchange yourself by undervaluing services you provide to the LLC. If you spent ten hours reading this book and forming your LLC, include that in your capital contributions by giving yourself a reasonable hourly "wage" for that work.

» **Additional Contributions by Members**: This provision spells out the terms under which members may need to contribute additional capital. New businesses typically need fresh influxes of cash from time to time until they become profitable. Failing to address the circumstances under which everyone must pitch in to keep the business going can result in one or more people contributing more than the others, which can change the ownership percentages and power dynamic.

» **Failure to Make Contributions**: There must be a procedure in place to deal with the situation of an LLC member failing to make their required capital contributions to the LLC. This provision states the consequences of that failure, including the potential to remove from membership a member who fails to contribute their required amount of capital.

» **No Interest on Capital Contributions**: This simple stipulation makes it clear that members will not receive interest on any funds or property contributed as capital to the LLC. Without this provision, state law might require simple interest to accumulate on capital contributions.

» **Capital Account Bookkeeping**: This establishes that the LLC will set up a capital account and maintain books regarding the details of that account. The "capital account" refers to an official ledger or record in which the LLC records any changes. Each member should have records that keep track of contributions, distributions, etc.

» **Consent to Capital Contribution Withdrawals and Distributions**: This provision provides parameters for members who may wish to make withdrawals or receive distributions from their capital contributions. One common state law limit is that businesses cannot pay out distributions to members if the business is running at a loss.

» **Allocations of Profits and Losses:** Normally, each member shares in profits or losses depending on their share of ownership. Someone who owns 60 percent of the business will receive twice as much in profits as someone who owns 30 percent of the business. Likewise, the 60 percent owner will bear twice the amount if losses occur. You should also include a schedule for the distribution of profits.

» **Allocation and Distribution of Cash to Members:** This establishes how cash from the LLC's business operations or from the sale of its assets are to be distributed to members.

» **Allocation of Noncash Distributions:** This provision establishes guidelines for how property other than cash is to be divided among members.

» **Allocation and Distribution of Liquidation Proceeds:** At some point, the LLC may be liquidated in full, or an individual member may liquidate their interest in the LLC. This provision addresses the procedure to be followed in the event of full or partial liquidation.

Fifth Set of Provisions: Membership Withdrawal and Transfer Provisions of an LLC Operating Agreement

This next set of provisions deals with how members can leave the LLC. It is important because having a member withdraw their membership or transfer it to another person can be disruptive to the business.

» **Withdrawal of Members:** This provision specifies how far in advance a member must give written notice to the other members before withdrawing their membership in the LLC.

» **Restrictions on the Transfer of Membership:** An LLC member should not be permitted to transfer their membership to another person without the approval of all other members. This prevents the transfer of membership to a person with whom other members do not wish to work or have as part of the business.

Sixth Set of Provisions: Dissolution Provisions of an LLC Operating Agreement

This provision deals with the dissolution of the LLC.

» **Events That Trigger Dissolution of the LLC**: This section establishes what events can result in the dissolution of the LLC. They may include the death of a member, the expiration of the LLC's length of duration, the agreement by all members that the LLC should be dissolved, or the dissolution of the LLC by the state.

Seventh Set of Provisions: General Provisions of an LLC Operating Agreement

The final set of provisions is a bit of a mixed bag. It establishes procedure concerning officers, lays out what each member is authorized to do, cites which state's laws the LLC will be governed by, and deals with resolving disputes among members.

» **Officers**: While an LLC isn't required to have designated officers, it can help to ensure that everyone understands their roles in the business and the expectations others have of them. An officers provision states the offices designated in the LLC, such as president, vice president, secretary, treasurer, financial director, and budget manager, and whether or not those positions will be compensated.

» **Records**: This provision outlines what records must be kept at the LLC and what they should include. Most states require businesses to maintain their records in one central location, which is why this provision is necessary.

» **All Necessary Acts**: This simply states that the members and officers of the LLC are authorized to perform all the acts necessary to benefit the LLC and help its business operations proceed efficiently. This may need to be revised if you intend to have members who are acting solely as investors without any rights to management.

» **Indemnification**: Indemnification is the practice of having one party assume financial responsibility for the harm caused by another. Car insurance is a common example where one party (the insurance company) agrees to assume financial responsibility for harm caused by another (the driver) in exchange for something (insurance premiums). In the context of an operating agreement, indemnification refers to the LLC promising to be financially responsible for harm caused by its members while they work on the company's behalf.

» **Mediation and Arbitration of Disputes Among Members**: This provision gives members of an LLC the opportunity to resolve problems among themselves without taking the matter to court. You don't need to specify this in your operating agreement, but most of my clients prefer to use *mediation*, which is when a third party works with partners to try to resolve a dispute, or *arbitration*, which is essentially a private trial overseen by an arbitrator instead of a judge. These methods keep disputes private as members work toward a resolution. Otherwise, a lawsuit may be the only way to resolve issues, and lawsuits are generally public record. As mentioned, public records can be a treasure trove of personal and business information that most people would rather not expose if they had a choice, because competitors, scammers, and disgruntled customers could use it to harass or harm their business. With this provision, you can choose to limit the information that gets out by electing to keep your disagreements behind closed doors.

» **Governing Law**: Your LLC can be governed by the laws of any state you choose, provided you have some kind of connection to the state. I prefer to use the state of formation, as it's less complicated.

» **Entire Agreement**: This provision is known as an "integration clause." The operating agreement is a contract between members of the LLC. This provision does two things: it limits how and when the operating agreement can be modified, and it omits any agreements or terms negotiated previously that are not within the document itself.

» **Severability**: If a state law changes and makes one or more provisions of your operating agreement unenforceable, this severability clause ensures that the agreement—with the exception of the provisions that have become unenforceable—is still valid. Without this clause, the entire agreement could be considered void because of the unenforceable provision.

Signatures: The Final Part of an LLC Operating Agreement

The final part of the operating agreement is the signatures of members, which are necessary for the agreement to be adopted. Signatures should be witnessed and accompanied by the printed name of each member and the date on which they signed.

Not every operating agreement will contain all the information I've mentioned, and some agreements may include provisions I haven't covered. Consider what applies to your LLC and the rules you'll need to ensure that the business runs smoothly.

Keeping Your Operating Agreement Up to Date

Just like your business, your operating agreement is a fluid document that is likely to change over time. New members might join your LLC, or you might add products or services and want to specify them in the agreement. Maybe you'll decide to hire a manager, thereby changing the company's management structure. It's a good idea to review your LLC's operating agreement after any significant company event and amend it as needed.

Ideally, your operating agreement will contain a provision outlining how you can change it. It might stipulate whether you need the consent of every member to make changes, or just a majority. All the members must come to a consensus on how changes will be made and put that information into a written document, with members signing to confirm their consent. The document then becomes part of the main operating agreement.

Chapter Recap

» An operating agreement helps keep everyone in accord regarding the rules that govern the LLC and adds an extra layer of protection from liability.

» Operating agreements are important for LLCs of all sizes and can be especially beneficial for single-member LLCs.

» An operating agreement is not a one-size-fits-all document, but one that should be tailored to the characteristics and needs of your LLC.

» Just like a business, an operating agreement is likely to change and will need to be updated from time to time.

| 7 |

Deciding How Your LLC Will Be Taxed

Chapter Overview
- » How Your LLC Is Taxed
- » Dealing with the IRS
- » Minimizing Taxes
- » Separating Personal and Business Finances

Tax laws as they apply to LLCs can seem strange, but once you understand how they work it's likely you'll appreciate the flexibility they provide. Due to something called *entity classification regulations*—rules that were established by the US Department of the Treasury in 1997—LLCs and certain other types of businesses can decide for themselves how they will be treated for tax purposes.

This flexibility is the result of how truly novel the LLC is. Limited liability companies only came into existence in 1977, through the Wyoming state legislature, as an attempt to provide entrepreneurs with a business entity that granted the same personal liability protection that corporations enjoyed while also allowing for the flexibility of a sole proprietorship. Between 1977 and 1997, several legal battles were fought over how LLCs should be taxed. The result is the system we have now by which LLCs can choose between several options for how they will be taxed, each with its own advantages and disadvantages.

Electing a tax status has become known as "checking the box." Form 8832—the one that allows selection of a tax preference for your LLC— includes a series of checkboxes, as seen in figure 10. If you don't elect how you want your LLC to be taxed, the IRS taxes it on its default entity classification, which is based on the number of members it has.

In this chapter, you'll learn about how LLCs are taxed and how an LLC's owner can change the way the LLC is treated for tax purposes by notifying the IRS. One disclaimer: Tax laws can change. What you'll read in this chapter is current at the time of publication, but it always makes sense to double-check the IRS's website when taking action that could affect your taxes.

IMAGE

fig. 10

Form 8832 (Rev. 12-2013)   Page **2**

Part I   Election Information (Continued)

6   **Type of entity** (see instructions):

a   ☐ A domestic eligible entity electing to be classified as an association taxable as a corporation.
b   ☐ A domestic eligible entity electing to be classified as a partnership.
c   ☐ A domestic eligible entity with a single owner electing to be disregarded as a separate entity.
d   ☐ A foreign eligible entity electing to be classified as an association taxable as a corporation.
e   ☐ A foreign eligible entity electing to be classified as a partnership.
f   ☐ A foreign eligible entity with a single owner electing to be disregarded as a separate entity.

7   If the eligible entity is created or organized in a foreign jurisdiction, provide the foreign country of
     organization ▶ ....

8   Election is to be effective beginning (month, day, year) (see instructions) . . . . ▶ _____

9   Name and title of contact person whom the IRS may call for more information | **10** Contact person's telephone number

IRS Form 8832, commonly referred to as the "check the box" form.

The First Step: Get an EIN

Before considering the options available for LLC taxation, you should apply for an employer identification number (EIN) if you have not already done so. Your EIN is important even if you do not have a single employee. Much like how we use our social security numbers as a means of identification, a business uses its EIN as an individual identification number in several different circumstances. Perhaps most important, the IRS requires you to have an EIN to file your taxes.

Generally, as you read in chapter 4, the IRS requires a sole proprietorship or partnership to get a new EIN when its ownership or structure changes. It's important to do this because the IRS uses your EIN to identify your business when it pays taxes, and other government and financial agencies rely on the number for other purposes, such as when your company applies for credit or opens a company bank account.

If your business is located in the United States or a US territory, you can apply for an EIN online. The person applying, known as the *responsible party*, needs to have a valid taxpayer identification number (TIN). The TIN can be a previous EIN or a Social Security number. Someone without a Social Security number would need to have an individual tax ID number, which is another form of tax processing number issued by the IRS, often to immigrants who haven't yet been issued a Social Security number.

NOTE

The responsible party, which is the individual who applies for the EIN, must be the person who owns or controls the business.

Once you start to fill out IRS Form SS-4, the online application for an EIN number, you need to complete it in one session. You cannot save it and come back to it later; your session expires after fifteen minutes of inactivity. However, if that happens, you can start over without penalty.

If the application is correctly completed, you should receive your EIN immediately after you submit your application. If, for some reason, you cannot complete the application online, you can fax or mail it to the IRS. This increases the processing time, of course. If you fax your application, it will take about four business days to receive your EIN. If you mail the application, you'll receive your EIN in about four weeks.

How the IRS Treats an LLC

You read a bit about how the IRS treats an LLC in chapter 2, but it's well worth a closer look. Unless you specify otherwise, the IRS defaults to taxing a single-member LLC as a sole proprietorship. A multimember LLC is taxed by default as a partnership. Most of the discussion in this chapter deals with federal taxes, but state and local taxes are also a consideration for LLCs. Like other types of businesses, LLCs are subject to state and local income taxes, and some states charge a separate LLC tax. California, for instance, levies an $800 annual LLC tax in addition to a fee that's based on an LLC's annual income. Generally, though, state and local tax laws mirror federal laws regarding how LLCs are taxed. State and local tax forms are more or less equivalent to IRS forms.

Single-Member LLCs

As the only member of an LLC, you report your income and expenses on Form 1040, Schedule C, just as a sole proprietor would do. Your business doesn't file the taxes; you do. Your taxes are based on your personal income rate, as indicated in figure 11, which shows tax brackets for the 2023 tax year, to be filed in 2024.

As you read in chapter 6, an LLC with one member is classified by the IRS as a disregarded entity, which is a business entity that is not considered to be separate from its owner and is "overlooked" for federal income tax purposes. The IRS, of course, is not going to let you get out of paying taxes, so you're required to report your LLC's profits on your individual tax return. So much for being "disregarded"!

However, there are some advantages to being classified as a disregarded entity, even if the term might sound a little degrading. You enjoy the benefits of *pass-through taxation*, which means that the LLC's profits are passed through to your individual tax return and taxed at your individual rate. That enables you to avoid double taxation, which occurs when a business pays tax at the corporate level and each owner's income is taxed at the personal level. Before LLCs were introduced, the only way to set up a company that could offer personal liability protection was to form a corporation. The corporate structure is great for some companies, but it's not the best business entity for everyone. Having a single-member LLC that's classified as a disregarded entity gives you personal liability protection without the downside of double taxation. If your LLC has losses for the year, they too can be passed through and used to offset other income you might have, such as portfolio income or income from another job.

GRAPHIC

fig. 11

FEDERAL INCOME TAX BRACKET FOR 2023
(FILING DEADLINE APRIL 15, 2024)

	SINGLE	MARRIED FILING JOINTLY	MARRIED FILING SEPARATELY	HEAD OF HOUSEHOLD
10%	$0 - $11,000	$0 - $22,000	$0 - $11,000	$0 - $15,700
12%	$11,001 - $44,725	$22,001 - $89,450	$11,001 - $44,725	$15,701 - $59,850
22%	$44,726 - $95,375	$89,451 - $190,750	$44,726 - $95,375	$59,851 - $95,350
24%	$95,376 - $182,100	$190,751 - $364,200	$95,376 - $182,100	$95,351 - $182,100
32%	$182,101 - $231,250	$364,201 - $462,500	$182,101 - $231,250	$182,101 - $231,250
35%	$231,251 - $578,125	$462,501 - $693,750	$231,251 - $346,875	$231,251 - $578,100
37%	$578,126 +	$11,001 - $44,725	$346,876 +	$578,101 +

Having to file only your personal tax return saves the time and expense of filing a separate return for your LLC. And, because disregarded entity status is imposed only at the federal level—not at the state level—the state continues to recognize your LLC as an entity separate from you, assuring you the protection from personal liability that an LLC provides.

Now that you've considered some advantages of having a disregarded entity, or single-member LLC, let's consider a pretty significant disadvantage. As the owner of a single-member LLC, you're responsible for paying self-employment taxes, which can take a chunk out of your earnings. When you're employed by someone else, you pay half of the required Social Security and Medicare taxes and your employer pays the other half. But because the IRS views the owner of a single-member LLC as both employee and employer, you have to pay both parts of those taxes, which in 2023 amounted to 15.3 percent. You can deduct half of what you pay in self-employment tax when calculating your *adjusted gross income*, which is your total gross income minus specific deductions permitted by the IRS, but self-employment taxes are still bothersome for many LLC owners.

Multimember LLCs

If your LLC has more than one member, you're taxed by default as a partnership. Like a single-member LLC, a multimember LLC is subject to pass-through taxation, which means the LLC itself doesn't pay taxes. Instead, the members pay them in accordance with their individual tax brackets.

Each year, a multimember LLC is required to file an informational return, Form 1065, US Return of Partnership Income. The business files a Form 1065, but each LLC member indicates their share of partnership income, credits, and deductions on Schedule K-1 and pays taxes on their share of profits. If two owners have a 50-50 ownership split, each pays taxes on half of the LLC's profits or gets to write off 50 percent of its losses. If five owners each have 20 percent ownership, each pays taxes on 20 percent of profits or writes off 20 percent of losses. LLC members attach their Schedule K-1s to their personal income tax returns.

As with a single-member LLC, owners of a multimember LLC avoid double taxation. And having to file only individual income tax returns simplifies the process, saving time and money. But members of a multimember LLC also have to pay those hefty self-employment taxes.

Choosing Corporate Tax Status for Your LLC

If you're tired of paying self-employment taxes or want to avoid having profits earned by your LLC affect your personal tax returns, you can choose to have your LLC classified as a corporation for tax purposes. All LLC members need to vote and agree to do this, and the change must be reflected in your LLC operating agreement.

LLCs are unique in that the owner of an LLC can specify to the IRS how they want the LLC to be taxed. No other business entity has that level of flexibility. In this QuickClip, I explain more about how to make use of it.

To watch the QuickClip, use the camera on your mobile phone to scan the QR code or visit the link below.

or

www.quickclips.io/llc-5

SCAN ME   VISIT URL

NOTE

If you (and the other members of your LLC if it's a multimember LLC) decide that you want your LLC to be treated as a corporation for tax purposes, the LLC remains an LLC from a legal standpoint. You still benefit from being able to choose how it's owned and managed, and it is subject to fewer regulations, such as the need to hold an annual shareholder's meeting, director's meetings, and so forth. You simply pay taxes the same way a corporation does.

You can elect to have your LLC taxed as a C corp, or, if it meets certain qualifications that enable the IRS to give it special tax status, as an S corp. To be designated as an S corp, it must meet the following criteria:

» It can have no more than one hundred shareholders.
» All shareholders must be residents of the United States.
» It can have only one class of stock.
» It cannot be owned by another corporation, LLC, or trust.

A downside of paying taxes as a C corp is that both the corporation and its shareholders are taxed on any income that's generated. The corporation must pay corporate income tax before any dividends can be distributed to shareholders, and shareholders are taxed on the income they receive from those dividends. That's the double taxation you read about earlier. Also, shareholders are not permitted to deduct business losses on their tax returns.

Unlike a C corp, an S corp isn't taxed on its earnings. Earnings are passed through to owners, who report them on their personal tax returns and are taxed accordingly. This avoids the double taxation of a C corp. And owners in an S corp are permitted to deduct business losses on their tax returns.

Tax Benefits of a C corp

While C corps face the issue of double taxation, there are some potential benefits of being taxed as a C corp. The 21 percent flat tax rate a corporation pays is lower than the income tax rate of many individuals. That makes the tax rate beneficial for the company. And even though the owners have to pay personal income tax on their earnings, they are not required to pay self-employment tax, because they are considered employees of the corporation.

C corps can also benefit from a variety of deductions, and they can take more operating losses than an LLC or S corp can and carry those losses over several years without attracting attention from the IRS. A C corp can take advantage of tax write-offs like medical reimbursement plans or disability insurance for employees and can deduct salaries as payroll taxes on its tax returns.

These and other advantages make the tax treatment of C corps attractive to some LLCs looking to change the way they are taxed.

Tax Benefits of an S Corp

In an S corp, owners can split their incomes between a shareholder distribution and a salary they receive as an employee of the business. An owner must pay taxes on the money earned as salary, including self-employment tax. However, no self-employment tax is levied on the money members receive as distributions. This gives employees a tax advantage. For example, let's say you anticipate the business to generate $100,000 in profit in year one. If your company is not an S corp, you would owe 15.3 percent in payroll taxes—approximately $15,300. If you were taxed as an S corp and paid yourself a "reasonable" salary of $50,000, you would owe payroll taxes only on that $50,000 (which would amount to $7,650). The remaining $50,000 would still be taxed, but it would not be subject to payroll taxes.

That ability to split the income and reduce the amount for which they pay self-employment tax has caused problems for more than one S corp owner. The IRS requires that a member of an S corp who works in the business must be paid a reasonable salary but does not define "reasonable" or stipulate what percentage of earnings must be considered salary rather than shareholder distribution. That makes it tempting to declare only a small part of your earnings as income to avoid paying more self-employment tax.

Be aware that the IRS tends to keep a close eye on S corps, recognizing the potential for abuse. Declaring a salary that is less than what a similar business would pay an employee can raise red flags with the IRS and trigger an audit. If you are caught lying or otherwise being dishonest with the IRS, they can—and will—impose substantial penalties and could even charge you with a federal crime.

Also, keep in mind that minimizing your payroll taxes by taking a low salary can have unexpected consequences. For example, your Social Security benefits are based on how much you contributed in Social Security taxes; therefore, minimizing your taxes will have an impact on the benefits you receive when you reach retirement age. Also, your "reasonable salary" may affect how you qualify for personal credit, such as when buying a home or car.

Another advantage of S corp tax status is that, in addition to normal deductions for business expenses, an owner can claim a 20 percent tax deduction on their share of business income. This is called the Qualified Business Income (QBI) deduction, and it's calculated on the owner's income as an employee. Sole proprietorships, partnerships, and LLCs also qualify for the QBI deduction. Generally, qualified business income refers to the net profit your business generates.

There are stipulations that apply to the QBI deduction, including that it does not apply to personal service businesses like engineering, health care, architecture, law, or accounting. Also, the deduction may be limited or unavailable to higher-income business owners.

In 2023, a single filer earning $170,050 or more or a joint filer earning $364,200 or more cannot qualify for the QBI deduction.

There are tax advantages associated with both C corps and S corps, along with some disadvantages. Deciding how your LLC will be taxed is a decision you should make only after careful consideration of all the pros and cons. If in doubt, use the default taxation option—disregarded entity for single-member LLCs and partnership for multimember LLCs. It can always be changed later once you get your business up and running.

Notifying the IRS of How You Elect to Be Taxed

If the members of your LLC decide to change your LLC's tax status to that of a corporation, get an IRS Form 8832 and check the box indicating the desired tax status. You may have filed this when you formed your LLC. Most LLC owners don't, which allows the IRS to assign them the default tax status of disregarded entity or partnership. So if you haven't filed a Form 8832, now's the time to do it. If you've already filed one electing to be taxed as an LLC, you'll have to refile to indicate that you now wish to be taxed as a corporation.

Remember that electing to have your LLC taxed as a corporation does not mean you are converting your LLC into a corporation. If, for some reason, you decided to change from an LLC to a corporation for management and/or organizational purposes, you would need to notify the state that you were formally changing the type of business entity. That would require further paperwork and, of course, fees.

If you change your tax status from an LLC to a corporation and indicate that decision on Form 8832, you'll normally be required to maintain your new status for five years—sixty months. There are exceptions to this rule, but it's something to consider if you're thinking about changing your LLC's status.

Filing Your Tax Returns

Filing federal tax returns is rarely enjoyable. It's a necessary task, however, and I think it's important to understand what's required so your taxes get filed properly and on time, regardless of whether you file as a disregarded entity, partnership, C corp, or S corp.

If you are new to running a business, I recommend using Intuit's QuickBooks for tracking expenses and income. If you use TurboTax, Intuit's tax preparation software, your income, expenses, mileage, and so forth can be pulled in to TurboTax directly from QuickBooks. And based on that information, TurboTax will try to find appropriate deductions and credits, which minimizes the amount of work you need to do at tax time.

Filing as a Sole Proprietorship

As mentioned, if your LLC is taxed as a sole proprietorship, you report your income and expenses each year on Form 1040, along with a Schedule C and a Schedule SE, and you pay estimated self-employment taxes quarterly.

While some business owners can claim income tax payments as expenses, sole proprietors may not. However, because the IRS does not distinguish between your personal and business income, you can have your business fund your tax payments. Do this by putting aside a percentage of business income to cover the taxes when they come due.

You can deduct business expenses on your return, but be sure to do some homework to find out what percentage of what expenses are fair game. Some expenses, like office equipment, business utility bills, and business travel, are 100 percent deductible, but you may be able to deduct only a certain percentage of other types of expenses.

Make sure to take advantage of some important deductions that can save you a lot of money. If you are not covered by a group benefits plan, you can deduct health insurance premiums for yourself and your family. This is advantageous because you can deduct it before arriving at your adjusted gross income, lowering the amount of income you'll have to pay tax on.

If you use your personal vehicle for business, be sure to claim the business mileage deduction, which in 2023 is 65.5 cents per mile. You can see how that adds up if you drive a lot for work. You can also deduct 50 percent of self-employment taxes, which takes some of the sting out of having to fund both the employer and employee sides of that tax.

The IRS provides a list of all taxes a sole proprietorship may be liable for, along with the forms needed to file each of them. Make sure you know what you're accountable for by checking the IRS website. Depending on the nature of your business, you could be responsible for taxes such as payroll taxes, property taxes, or sales taxes.

Also pay attention to when your returns must be filed. Some returns, like Form 1040 and Schedule C, are filed annually, and others, like Form 941 for payroll taxes, must be filed quarterly. Not filing and paying your taxes on time can result in penalties.

Schedule C is fairly easy to complete, but one topic might be unfamiliar: you'll be asked to indicate what accounting method your business employs. Most business owners who do their own bookkeeping use *cash-based accounting*, which is a method that recognizes income and expenses when they're received. Revenue is reported only when cash is received, and expenses are recorded when cash is paid out. It's likely your business employs a cash-based accounting system, which you'll indicate on Schedule C.

An alternative to cash-based accounting is *accrual accounting*. This system records revenue when a product or service is delivered to a customer—not when cash for the product or service is received. Expenses for goods and services are recorded at the time they are ordered or acquired, not when bills for them come due and cash is paid out.

If you do your own taxes, take your time and be certain of the taxes you're responsible for, as well as how to fill out the forms.

Filing as a Partnership

If your LLC is taxed as a partnership, the business will need to file a Form 1065, US Return of Partnership Income, every year. Each member of the partnership will file a Schedule K-1 along with their Form 1040. While 1065 and K-1 forms are filed annually, it's common for partners to pay quarterly estimated taxes.

The partnership's total income or loss is reported on Form 1065, along with deductions. Pay attention to the deductions you're entitled to as an LLC taxed as a partnership: salaries, rent, some taxes, employee benefit programs, guaranteed payments to partners, repairs, and others.

The partnership will also have to file several Form 1065 schedules, most likely a Schedule B that includes a list of questions about the partnership, a Schedule K detailing income and expenses, and a Schedule L, which is a balance sheet. Form 1065 must be signed by a general partner and submitted with the schedules.

The partnership must complete a Schedule K-1 for anyone who was a partner at any time during the tax year. Schedule K-1 forms, which include partners' names, addresses, and percentage shares of profits and losses, must be distributed to all partners by March 15 of the filing year, because the partners need the forms to prepare their personal tax returns. The partnership also files copies of the K-1 forms along with Form 1065.

Partnerships are likely to be required to file state, as well as federal, tax returns. Depending on where your partnership is based, it may be levied franchise, excise, or sales taxes. Each partner must report their share of partnership income or loss—as provided on the K-1 form—on their federal tax return. Partnership income for a general partner, meaning a partner who is actively involved in running the business, is typically considered self-employment income, for which a Form SE needs to be filed. Income received by limited partners, those who aren't actively involved in running the business, is considered passive income and not subject to self-employment tax.

Filing as a C Corporation

If you've elected to have your LLC taxed as a C corp, filing your taxes is likely to be more complicated than if it is taxed as a sole proprietorship or a partnership. A C corp is taxed as a separate entity and must file a Form 1120, US Corporation Income Tax Return, yearly. The income a corporation earns is typically taxed at the corporate level, which is currently a flat rate of 21 percent.

Form 1120 requires you to provide information about the corporation including its total assets, date of incorporation, legal name and address, and so forth. You must give a breakdown of income by category, including capital gains, cost of goods sold, dividends, interest, rents, and royalties.

Deductions are included on Form 1120. Be sure you have documentation for any deductions you claim, such as officer compensation and other wages and salaries, rents, charitable contributions, employee benefit programs, taxes, licenses, bad debt, maintenance and repairs, and interest expense. Some deductions, such as depreciation, require a separate form.

After the corporation pays taxes on its profits, shareholders who received distributions from those profits will need to pay taxes on the same money on their personal tax returns—hence the double taxation to which corporations are subject.

Corporations are likely to pay state income tax, which is usually a flat percentage that varies from state to state. Currently, forty-four states levy a corporate income tax, ranging from 2.5 percent in North Carolina to 11.5 percent in New Jersey. Nevada, Ohio, Texas, and Washington impose gross receipts taxes instead of corporate income taxes, and a few states impose gross receipts taxes in addition to corporate income taxes. A corporation may face additional state taxes if it's registered to do business in more than one state.

C corps must pay estimated corporate income tax at scheduled times throughout the year. As with other business entities, not paying estimated taxes on time can result in penalties and interest payments.

Filing as an S Corporation

The earnings of an S corp are passed through to its owners, who report them on their personal tax returns and are responsible for paying taxes on those earnings. Similar to a C corp, an S corp reports its company financial activity on Form 1120-S and must complete and attach a Schedule K-1 for each shareholder.

Each shareholder gets a copy of their Schedule K-1, which includes their share of the business's taxable income to be reported on their personal tax returns. An S corp must file its previous year's tax return by March 15, unless that date lands on a weekend or holiday (in which case the return is due the next business day). Shareholders filing K-1 forms must file them—along with their individual tax returns—by April 15, the IRS deadline for individual taxpayers.

An S corp that pays salaries to employees is responsible for withholding federal income tax, Social Security, and Medicare taxes from employee paychecks. The S corp files an IRS Form 941 quarterly to report the amount that has been withheld and must be submitted to the IRS. The S corp may also have to file an annual Form 940, Federal Unemployment Tax Return.

S corps that don't file their 1120-S forms on time have to pay a specified penalty each month they are late, multiplied by the number of shareholders. The minimum penalty in 2022 was $210 for each month or part of a month that the return is late. That can add up to a significant sum for an S corp with a large number of shareholders.

Minimizing What You Owe

While nearly all businesses have to pay taxes, there are some ways you can minimize what you owe, regardless of whether your LLC is taxed as a sole proprietorship, partnership, C corp, or S corp. One of those strategies is obvious: take advantage of any and all deductions to which you're entitled. You've read about some possible deductions in this chapter, such as health insurance premiums, business use of a personal vehicle, a portion of your self-employment taxes, and the QBI deduction that applies to some LLCs.

Many LLC owners and prospective owners don't realize that many start-up expenses are tax-deductible. If you're getting ready to launch an LLC or are in the process of doing so, consider some expenses you might be able to deduct from your income taxes:

> » **Business planning**. If you travel to check out possible business locations or spend time researching the potential labor market or customer base or the viability of products and services you plan to offer, these costs may be deductible.

> » **Business equipment and services**. Business equipment and costs for services such as marketing consultants, advertising, and other expenses incurred as you are getting ready to launch your LLC can be deducted from your taxes.

> » **Business organization**. An LLC with two or more members can deduct the costs of organizational fees paid to the state, costs of business meetings, legal fees, and other expenses related to getting the business up and running.

There are limits to start-up deductions, of course, so make sure you research exactly what is permitted and what is not. If your LLC has two or more members and you spend $50,000 or less on start-up costs, you can claim up to $5,000 in deductions. Because most small businesses don't generate a lot of profit in their first year of business, you can amortize—or spread out—your start-up costs over a period of time, generally fifteen years.

Single-member LLCs, unfortunately, are not permitted to amortize start-up costs. However, if your LLC has only one member and you spend $5,000 or less on start-up expenses, you are permitted to deduct up to $5,000 in organizational costs in your first year.

You also can reduce your tax bill by maximizing your retirement savings, as permitted by law. If you own a single-member LLC and are considered self-employed, you can set up a single-participant 401(k) plan, which allows you to save up to 100 percent of your income as an employee contribution. The limit on income you can contribute was $61,000 in 2022, or $67,500 if you're fifty or older. Contributing money to a 401(k) reduces your taxable income, which in turn lowers your tax.

If a single-participant 401(k) plan, often called a solo 401(k), isn't appropriate, you can consider a SIMPLE IRA or a SEP IRA plan, which can also help you reduce and defer taxes. A SIMPLE (Savings Incentive Match Plan for Employees) IRA plan enables employers and employees to contribute to traditional IRAs that have been set up for employees. These plans are recommended as start-up retirement savings plans for businesses that have a small number of employees and don't offer a company-wide retirement plan.

The SEP IRA is intended to make it easy for someone who is self-employed or a small business owner to benefit from tax-advantaged plans. Those who are eligible for a SEP (Simplified Employee Pension) IRA can contribute up to 25 percent of net earnings from self-employment, or an employer can contribute up to 25 percent of an employee's total compensation, as long as that percentage doesn't exceed a certain amount.

There is plenty of information available about choosing the right retirement plan to help you save money and minimize your taxes. Be sure to do some research before you set up an account, and consider consulting an accountant or financial advisor.

Keeping Personal and Business Finances Separate

Whichever legal entity you choose for your company, you should take care to keep your business and personal finances separate. An LLC or corporation is a separate legal entity with its own financial system, but separating personal and business accounts is also advisable for sole proprietorships and partnerships, which, as you know, are not considered separate from their owners. Consider this advice from the US Small Business Administration:

» **Establish a small business bank account**. Keep your personal and business funds in two different bank accounts and use separate checking accounts. That will ensure your funds remain separate and makes it easier to maintain a clean and efficient bookkeeping system.

» **Get a business credit card**. Use this card for everything you charge that's business-related, as it allows you to track expenses, analyze spending, and build your business credit. It's also helpful at tax time, as you won't need to separate your personal and business expenditures.

» **Apply for a data universal number system (DUNS) number.** The most widely used identifying number for US businesses, the Data Universal Number System (DUNS) was established by the business data firm Dun & Bradstreet (D&B) in the 1960s. It's free to US businesses, and it enables you to build a business credit identity that's separate from your personal credit history.

» **Set up separate utility accounts.** Set up accounts for business phones, cell phone service, internet service and other utilities used to operate your business in the company's name. Apply for credit in the LLC's name. If you apply for credit with a supplier or vendor, use your LLC information on the credit application. This allows your LLC to establish a credit history and may enable you to get extended financing terms from the suppliers and vendors you deal with.

Chapter Recap

» If you don't indicate to the IRS how you want your LLC to be taxed, the IRS will, by default, tax a single-member LLC as a sole proprietorship and a multiple-member LLC as a partnership.

» The members of an LLC can elect to have the LLC taxed as a corporation, but they must notify the IRS of this decision.

» Filing tax returns can be challenging and time-consuming, so it's important to understand which tax forms, rules, and deadlines apply to your LLC.

» You can save money on taxes by taking advantage of strategies to minimize them.

» Maintaining separate personal and business finances is important for any type of business entity.

| 8 |

Deciding on a Management Structure

Chapter Overview
» LLC Managers Run the Daily Operations of the Business
» Skills and Expertise Are Necessary Qualities of Managers
» Pros and Cons of Different Management Structures
» Responsibilities of LLC Managers

Determining how your LLC will be managed is an important decision, as your management structure affects the day-to-day operations of the business and can have an impact on your tax situation. As you've read, you and other members get to decide whether your LLC will be member-managed or manager-managed. There are three options for managing an LLC:

» Management by *all* members
» Management by one or more members but not all
» Management by a nonmember

In a member-managed LLC, *all* members have equal rights in managing the daily operations of the business. That model is the default management structure in some states; it is also the default model for a single-member LLC.

In a manager-managed LLC, the LLC designates either an outside professional or one or more members—but not all—to run the business. If you decide on a manager-managed LLC, you'll need to inform the state of your decision, because the default setting in most states is member management. In states without a default rule, your certificate of formation/articles of organization will likely be rejected if you do not specify your LLC's management structure in the document.

A question I commonly get asked is, "Why do I have to choose between 'member-managed' and 'manager-managed'?" The answer lies in public policy. Third parties—such as banks, vendors, and service providers—need to know who has the power to bind the LLC to agreements. If your LLC is member-managed, third parties know all members have equal rights to management and so they know any member can enter into an agreement on behalf of the LLC. If the LLC is manager-managed, third parties know to inquire further to make sure whoever is in front of them has the power to open a bank account, buy inventory, or hire someone on behalf of the company.

Although I discuss both the member-managed and manager-managed methods of running an LLC in this chapter, I strongly discourage you from handing over the duties of managing your LLC to a professional manager. There are reasons why some LLCs decide to do this, but in my opinion it's just too risky to give control of your business to someone who's not a member. If you absolutely cannot handle the day-to-day duties of running your company, you can hire an employee to act as a manager without naming him or her as a manager in your certificate of formation / articles of organization. Doing this gives you the flexibility to delegate the management of the business without giving someone sweeping powers over the business entity itself.

What Does Managing an LLC Involve?

LLC managers have many responsibilities involved with running the day-to-day operations of the company. This can include tasks such as signing contracts on behalf of the business, managing financial affairs, handling marketing, and buying real estate and other property. Basically, a manager interacts with third parties and the general public, handling decisions and overseeing operations.

Before you agree to take on management responsibilities for your LLC, you should make sure you have a solid understanding of the work you'll be doing. Depending on what tasks you're responsible for, you'll need to understand how the terms of a contract work, how your LLC's financial affairs are structured, and the ins and outs of buying property. You'll need to open, close, and manage bank accounts, make sure all the bills are paid, hire (and possibly fire) employees and other staff members, and borrow money through a business loan. Don't assume that just because you've been named to the position of manager that you're equipped to handle every matter that comes along.

Ideally, if more than one member is managing the LLC, they have complementary backgrounds and skills that enable the effective running of daily operations. There may be times, however, when your LLC needs to consult professionals who can provide sound advice on complicated matters, especially when the stakes are high.

If your operating agreement names officer positions in your LLC, the people who hold those positions are not necessarily managers, although they can be. I'll use Jack and Miguel, the guys you met earlier in the book who own and run the food truck business, as an example. Let's say that Jack serves as president, Miguel as vice president, and both serve as managers.

Unlike a corporation, an LLC isn't legally required to have a board of directors or named officers, but it's not uncommon. How you choose to structure the management will depend a lot on the circumstances of your LLC. Jack and Miguel, for instance, have been cooking together since high school, always with the dream of starting and running a business together. They know each other well, understand their own and each other's strengths and weaknesses, and can work together effectively. It just makes sense for them to own and manage their business together. If it grows to the point where they have three food trucks heading out across a three-county area on any weekend day, they'll need to hire more employees and most likely another manager or two to maintain their business.

Let's take a closer look at two possible management structures for an LLC: member-managed and manager-managed, and the pros and cons of each.

Member-Managed vs. Manager-Managed

Your LLC can be member-managed or manager-managed, and members of the LLC get to choose the management structure they wish to have. Member-managed LLCs are more common than manager-managed ones, mostly because the majority of LLCs are small, every member wants an equal say in managing the business, and they don't need to hire a professional manager.

One of the primary advantages of member-managed LLCs is that they enable all owners to have an equal say in the day-to-day operations. Jack and Miguel, for example, work together to develop new dishes to add to their food truck offerings. Miguel handles day-to-day finances, while Jack takes charge of booking events and making sure they stay in compliance with the local zoning laws. They are partners when it comes to hiring employees, buying new equipment, and arranging for any needed repairs. Each knows his role and is good at what he does, and they work almost seamlessly together. They're living that dream they've had since high school, and it's working for them.

This scenario can also apply to LLCs with a greater number of members. Even if a member-managed LLC has twenty member-managers, each has an equal say in decisions about how the business is run. (Keep in mind that "equal rights" to management generally excludes ownership percentages.) If all members are managers, then they have equal rights to management. If a member's rights in managing the business are limited in any way, the business is manager-managed.

But let's say Jack and Miguel decide they really want to take their business to the next level. They find several investors who are willing to finance that expansion, but those investors don't know anything about running a food truck or any other type of food service operation and have no interest in doing so. The investors are handing over their money because they believe Jack and Miguel are capable of expanding the business and that they'll reap the benefits through a share of the profits.

Those investors are called *passive investors*. They are owners, or members, but they do not have any power to manage the business. In this case, Jack and Miguel could be named managers of the business in a legal sense, with their positions listed on the articles of organization and filed with the state, giving their LLC a manager-managed structure. That's because an LLC is considered member-managed only when every member shares management responsibilities equally. If some members are performing management duties and others are not, the LLC is considered manager-managed.

The operating agreement is where you would specify who are the "managing members" that have the power to manage the business and who are the "investor members" whose only rights extend to calling meetings, receiving distributions, and so forth, and who are excluded from having power to manage the business.

Another option would be for Jack and Miguel, and their passive investors to hire an outside manager to run the day-to-day operations. That would free up Jack and Miguel to attract still more investors if, say, they decided to add a full-fledged, 200-seat barbeque restaurant to their food truck operation. That manager, who would be legally recognized as an employee and work as an employee of the company, would be responsible for running the business on a daily basis without having to seek consensus from the owners. That type of situation can streamline the running of a business, since the manager is able to make decisions quickly but lacks the legal power to do things that could hurt the company, such as closing the LLC's bank account.

If the manager is someone who understands the business, has worked in the food service industry, comes with impeccable references, and is trustworthy to the max, Jack and Miguel and the other owners may feel completely comfortable with that person running the business while they work on expanding it.

fig. 12

MEMBER- VS MANAGER-MANAGED LLCS		
	MEMBER-MANAGED	**MANAGER-MANAGED**
Good for small memberships?	Yes	Not usually
Good for large memberships?	Not always	Yes
Simplicity	More streamlined	Less streamlined
Allows passive investment?	No	Yes
Attracting investors	Harder	Easier
Attracting qualified management	Harder	Easier
Decision-making speed	Slower	Faster
Member control	High	Low

Some pros and cons of member-managed and manager-managed LLCs

It bears repeating, however, that a manager-managed structure in which a nonmember runs your business can set you up to lose control of the organization, because it removes a large part of member control. For instance, a manager has legal authority to take out a loan on behalf of an LLC. If you unwittingly hire a manager who's a bad actor, it's possible for them to take out a big loan in the company's name and take off with it, leaving members of the LLC responsible for paying back money that's now funding their former manager's lifestyle on a tropical island. Also, a legal manager has nothing to lose except their job if the company fails, but members lose the money they invested in the company, along with all the time and effort they've put in.

You also need to pay the manager a salary, which means the LLC will owe payroll taxes. If you choose to have an outside manager listed in the articles of organization / certificate of formation for your LLC, it's vitally important to establish their rights and responsibilities in your operating agreement. Think carefully about how much control you're willing to hand over, and consider the pros and cons of the decision, remembering the reasons you wanted to start an LLC in the first place. If you're in doubt, I recommend that you simply hire an employee and name them as the manager, rather than give them the sweeping powers of a legal manager of the LLC.

Defining the Responsibilities of LLC Managers

If you're electing to have a member-managed LLC, it's important to understand what the management duties entail. Some typical duties are mentioned earlier in this chapter, but let's take a closer look at what's involved.

Maintaining Records

While recordkeeping for LLCs is less involved than for business entities such as corporations, there are still rules you must follow to maintain your LLC's limited liability status. The documents you'll need to keep depend on your state's laws. Normally, though, you should maintain the following records that pertain to your LLC's finances and organization:

» **Income tax returns**. Keep your LLC's federal, state, and local income tax returns for at least three years; that's the amount of time during which the IRS can conduct a routine audit. If fraud is suspected, there is no statute of limitation for an audit, so it's best to retain tax returns permanently.

» **Related financial records**. Any records showing expenses, income, or credits incurred by the LLC should be maintained. These could include paid bills, invoices, canceled checks, credit card statements, bank account deposit slips, and other documents.

» **Employment tax records**. If your LLC has employees, you'll have to pay federal income tax, Social Security, Medicare, and unemployment taxes, known collectively as employment taxes. You should keep information pertaining to these taxes, such as W-4 forms, copies of employee tax returns, employee payment records, records of employment such as time cards, and the name, address, Social Security number, and dates of employment for all employees. Keep these records for at least three years—ideally, ten.

» **Financial records and contracts.** Keep all financial statements and significant records and business contracts for at least six years.

» **Operating agreement.** You'll want to have this important document stored and available at your LLC's principal place of business, along with any documents that relate to it, such as a disciplinary warning to a member.

» **Member and manager information.** Keep an updated list of all members and managers, including full names, addresses, and dates of membership.

» **Minutes of meetings.** If meetings are required in your operating agreement or your LLC chooses to hold meetings for any reason, you should keep accurate records of what occurs at them. Include the names of everyone present, any votes or decisions that are made, and other information that documents the events of the meeting.

Maintaining Day-to-Day Operations

If you're a member-manager of an LLC, the daily tasks you perform can vary widely and might include everything from keeping track of cash flow to hauling out the trash. Daily operations will be different depending on the type of company you have, but they are likely to include some of the activities listed here:

» **Marketing.** Most businesses want people to know about them, which is typically accomplished through some sort of marketing effort. You might need to start and maintain social media accounts, establish branding for your company, create a marketing budget, and decide about advertising copy and venues.

» **Customer service.** You'll need customers and you'll want to keep them happy, which can involve responding to customer feedback, explaining how the business works, setting up appointments, and handling any special requests they might have.

» **Making and distributing your product.** If your LLC produces and distributes a product, there's no doing business without it. You'll need to keep equipment in working order, keep track of orders, plan for production, package and store the product, and make sure it gets to its destination.

> » **Keeping an eye on finances**. Money is important to any business. This means you'll need to keep track of purchasing, revenue, and accounts payable and receivable. You may be charged with obtaining capital, compiling financial reports, and generally dealing with the information contained in your financial reports.

> » **Purchasing supplies**. A business depends on certain supplies, so there must be inventory records to track what you have and what you need. Supplies must be ordered as required to continue providing your product or service.

Running Meetings

If your LLC holds meetings, you as a manager could be called on to chair them. Running a meeting isn't rocket science, but there are some things you should remember to help keep you on task and ensure that the meeting proceeds smoothly. Business experts recommend these steps for a successful meeting:

> » **Make sure everyone knows why they're there**. The purpose of the meeting should be clear to all attendees. Ideally, an agenda should be distributed in advance. It doesn't have to be anything fancy; an email with a couple of sentences about why you're gathering and what you expect to accomplish will convey a sense of purpose.

> » **Prepare any materials you'll need during the meeting**. If you need handouts or to be able to share your computer screen to display a spreadsheet, have everything ready to go before people arrive at the meeting. You don't want to delay the start of the meeting or have it disrupted because you're not prepared.

> » **Keep the meeting moving**. Avoid getting distracted or letting the conversation get sidetracked. Stick to the agenda items, be respectful of attendees' time, and end the meeting on time.

> » **Leave with a plan for action items**. Action items that are agreed on during the meeting should be assigned to the appropriate person or people before the meeting ends. Be sure everyone understands what is to be accomplished and by when.

If you've never chaired a meeting and find it difficult at first, rest assured that it will get easier. You'll gain confidence with experience, and the process will become much more like second nature.

Ensuring Tax Compliance

Make sure you know what forms you need, that they're filled out to the best of your ability, and that they get filed on time. And don't forget the importance of always keeping your personal and business finances separate, because not doing so can result in serious issues.

Managing Members and Employees

It's been firmly established that happy, hardworking, productive employees are better for a company than those who are disgruntled and unproductive, and the concept also applies to members of an LLC. There's a wealth of material available about management, and details about employee relations are beyond the scope of this book, but here are a few general tips from experts:

»   **Keep the lines of communication open**. Regardless of how many managers and/or employees your LLC has, everyone wants to know what's happening regarding ongoing projects, company objectives and goals, successes, and failures. I'm not saying that every person always needs to know everything, but all managers and/or employees, assuming they're engaged in their work and invested in the success of the business, will expect to be kept informed about important decisions and events. Also, all managers and/or employees should feel free to ask questions and express concerns and have those questions and concerns addressed by management.

»   **Give the right people the right jobs**. Members of an LLC possess varying skills, knowledge, and expertise, and each person is a better fit for certain tasks than for others. People are more likely to be successful doing tasks in which they feel confident and where they feel they're using their best abilities.

»   **Manage performance**. Meet one-on-one with managers and employees to discuss strengths and areas for improvement and how performance can be enhanced. Most people appreciate feedback, whether it's positive or constructive criticism.

» **Make sure everyone is on the same page**. People who work together, especially those with a share in a company, like LLC members, need to work as a team, with everyone on the same wavelength. Make sure each person understands their role within the company and what's expected of them. Clarifying these guidelines helps everyone to gauge how they're doing and when improvement is necessary.

» **Get to know each other**. Looking out for other LLC members or employees can go a long way in keeping people motivated and working to their potential. Make it a point to know about each other's families and interests outside of work, and check in if you know someone is going through a rough time. People appreciate being seen as humans as well as workers.

» **Encourage teamwork**. Most LLCs are small companies in which teamwork is especially important. Success is more likely if members understand the goals of the company and are working together to realize them.

Review of the Steps for Starting an LLC

Although each state has its own rules for how LLCs are established and maintained, the following list will, walk you through the steps that are necessary in most states.

1. Decide where to register your LLC.

2. Choose a name for your LLC.

3. Decide how your LLC will be managed.

4. Complete an articles of organization document. Include this information:
   • The name of your LLC
   • A statement of the purpose of the business
   • The name and address of the LLC's registered agent
   • An explanation of how the LLC will be managed
   • Address of the LLC

- How long the LLC will operate
- Names of members, managers, and directors of the LLC

5. File the Articles of Organization document with your state.

6. Receive your Certificate of Formation from your state.

7. Complete an Operating Agreement for your LLC. Include this information:

- **Preliminary Provisions**
  » Effective date
  » Formation (or statement of intent)
  » Name
  » Registered office and agent
  » Business purpose
  » Duration of the LLC

- **Membership Provisions**
  » Non-liability members
  » Reimbursement for organizational costs
  » Management
  » Members' percentage interest
  » Membership voting
  » Compensation
  » Members' meetings
  » Membership certificates
  » Other business by members

- **Tax and Financial Provisions**
  » LLC's tax classification
  » Tax year and accounting method
  » Tax matters partner
  » Annual income tax returns and reports
  » Bank accounts
  » Title to assets

- **Capital Provisions**
  » Capital contributions by members

- » Additional contributions by members
- » Failure to make contributions
- » No interest on capital contributions
- » Capital account bookkeeping
- » Consent to capital contribution withdrawals and distributions
- » Allocations of profits and losses
- » Allocation and distribution of cash to members
- » Allocation of noncash distributions
- » Allocation and distribution of liquidation proceeds

- **Membership Withdrawal and Transfer Provisions**
  - » Withdrawal of members
  - » Restrictions on the transfer of membership

- **Dissolution Provisions**
  - » Events that trigger dissolution of the LLC

- **General Provisions**
  - » Officers
  - » Records
  - » All necessary acts
  - » Indemnification
  - » Mediation and arbitration of disputes among members
  - » Governing law
  - » Entire agreement
  - » Severability

- **Signature of Members**

8. Apply for an Employer Identification Number for your LLC.

9. Select a corporate tax status for your LLC.

10. Notify the IRS of how you want your LLC to be taxed.

Chapter Recap

» In a member-managed LLC, it's important to understand the skills, knowledge, and expertise of each manager and how they can best be applied to the day-to-day operations of the company.

» Member-managed LLCs and manager-managed LLCs each have advantages and disadvantages; however, member management is almost always recommended for a small company.

» Member-managers of an LLC may need to perform a wide variety of tasks, so it is important to understand what those jobs entail.

PART III

THE LIFE CYCLE OF AN LLC

| 9 |

Managing Day-to-Day Operations

Chapter Overview
- » The Importance of Reports
- » The Corporate Veil
- » Licenses, Franchise Taxes, and Insurance
- » Changing Your Tax Structure
- » Expansion

Starting a business and running it yourself are exciting life experiences. So it's likely that after going through the process of filing articles of incorporation and drafting an operating agreement, you're eager to get down to the work of running your business and earning some money.

I hear you on that, but there are some important ongoing requirements you'll need to consider to make sure your LLC remains legally compliant. Local, state, and federal business laws vary depending on the type and location of a business. You should be aware of what they are and which ones apply to you.

There is a handy state-by-state LLC formation guide included in your Digital Assets. Access this and your other Digital Assets at go.quickstartguides.com/llc

In this chapter, we'll look at some of the things you may need to do to remain in compliance with the law. Check to see what's specific to the state where your LLC is registered. These are the guidelines you'll need to get started:

Filing Reports
Most states require an LLC to file an annual report detailing changes that have occurred in the business during a specified period of time. In addition, a handful of states require an *initial report*, often within ninety days of when the LLC is registered. The initial report, sometimes referred to as a statement of information, is a report filed in conjunction with the formation of an LLC.

It contains information such as the name and address of the LLC's registered agent, names and possibly addresses of LLC members and officers, and an explanation of the purpose of the business. An initial report is not the same as articles of organization, which are filed with the state to establish a business.

Alaska, California, Louisiana, Nevada, and Washington currently require LLCs to file initial reports, usually with a filing fee, within a specific time from when the business was registered.

An **annual report** is an update on your business that must be filed with the state in which your LLC is registered. You must report any changes in your LLC's address, ownership and officers, and/or registered agent. Some states require that you also provide information about earnings, assets, and stock.

As the report's name implies, most states, but not all, require these updates every year. Some states, including Nebraska, Indiana, New York, and California, require the reports every *other* year. Missouri, Ohio, and Arizona do not require LLCs to file annual reports.

Filing fees vary significantly from state to state, ranging from $9 in New York to $300 in Delaware, Maryland, and the District of Columbia. Idaho, Minnesota, Mississippi, and Texas require annual reports, but there is no filing fee. In Tennessee, it costs $300 to file a report for a single-member LLC; if there is more than one member, an extra $50 is added per member, up to a maximum fee of $3,000.

Failing to remain in compliance with annual report rules can have serious consequences. Not filing the report can result in your business being placed on revoked status, which is effectively an **annual report**.

This means the state takes away your ability to do business. It also means the business may no longer have limited liability protection—which is likely the very reason you formed an LLC in the first place. That, of course, opens you up to legal liability in the event of a lawsuit or debt and can result in what is called "piercing the veil," a process we'll learn more about in the next section of this chapter.

I once helped a client get a tattoo parlor set up and registered as an LLC in Texas. During a periodic check-in, I asked if she had filed her annual report with the state. She'd forgotten to do it, and she had to scramble to figure out who to contact and how to remedy the problem. Even though Texas doesn't charge a filing fee for the report, she owed a penalty for neglecting to file.

If you're late in filing the annual report, you'll face financial penalties. Some states send notifications to remind businesses that their annual reports are coming due, but others send no notification until the report is overdue. Keeping track of these due dates is up to you.

Piercing the Corporate Veil

One of the most appealing aspects of an LLC—and one of the primary reasons why entrepreneurs go to the effort and expense of forming them—is that they help avoid personal liability in the event of debt or a lawsuit. In fact, LLCs came into being largely because judges, legislators, and others recognized that the risk of losing everything if a business failed was a deterrent to entrepreneurs attempting to form them in the first place. Before LLCs, forming a corporation was the only way to limit personal liability in business, but corporations require significantly more formal procedures to remain compliant, and they subject owners to double taxation. To mitigate this, Wyoming devised the limited liability company, a business structure that largely shields owners from liability in the event of debt, breaches of contract, and personal injuries caused by the business or its owners, while providing flexibility in management options and avoiding double taxation.

There are certain cases in which an LLC member's personal assets are not protected, including when a member personally guarantees a business loan or obligation. Also, members cannot hide behind their LLC if they commit acts that cause intentional harm to another person, such as battery or fraud. And members who practice in a licensed profession, such as attorneys and doctors, are still liable for their professional negligence despite operating through an LLC.

But while limited liability for LLC members is a well-established and respected rule, it's not completely airtight. In certain instances, a person or business can come after your personal assets and the courts will rule in favor of piercing the corporate veil—the very scenario you formed the LLC to avoid.

Generally, single-member or small multimember LLCs are more vulnerable to veil piercing than large ones, for very simple reasons: an LLC with one, two, or three members is less likely to hold and record regular meetings, have an operating agreement or keep it updated, make sure the company runs in accordance with the operating agreement, never use company money for personal business, and so forth. Be aware of this and try to take every step possible to reduce the likelihood of having your corporate veil pierced.

Why Courts Pierce the Corporate Veil

For a court to pierce the LLC's corporate veil and decide that its members are personally liable, the business owners must have done—or failed to do—some specific things. These things include, but are not limited to, failing to treat the business as an entity separate from its owners, commingling personal funds and assets with business funds and assets, committing fraud or other illegal acts, and undercapitalizing the LLC when it is formed. These situations make it possible for a creditor to pierce the corporate veil, putting your personal assets at risk. Here are more details about these situations:

» **Not treating the business as an entity separate from its owners.** When you form an LLC, you must meet certain compliance regulations, such as obtaining business licenses, filing annual reports, holding business meetings, filing a fictitious name if applicable, creating bylaws, keeping records, documenting business actions, and so on. While a failure to do these things probably won't be the sole justification for piercing the veil, it can function as evidence for the courts that LLC members have not respected the fact that the business exists as a separate entity.

» **Commingling personal funds and assets with business funds and assets.** The commingling of personal funds and assets with business funds and assets is a real red flag for courts and a big reason why they might rule in favor of piercing the veil. Depositing checks made out to the LLC into a personal bank account, using money in an LLC account to pay personal bills, or using a company car for family vacations do not fly when there are legal issues involved.

» **Committing fraud or other illegal acts.** This is another area that courts do not look upon kindly. If you commit an unlawful act, defraud an individual or a business, or take out loans you know you can't repay, you're setting your LLC up for veil piercing.

» **Undercapitalizing the LLC when it is formed.** If you started doing business as an LLC without enough funds to properly support it, then you formed your company without enough start-up capital. This makes it easier for creditors to argue that your LLC is not sufficiently separate from its owners to warrant a corporate veil. A business owner must assess how much capital is needed to cover initial costs and liabilities, including payments to creditors.

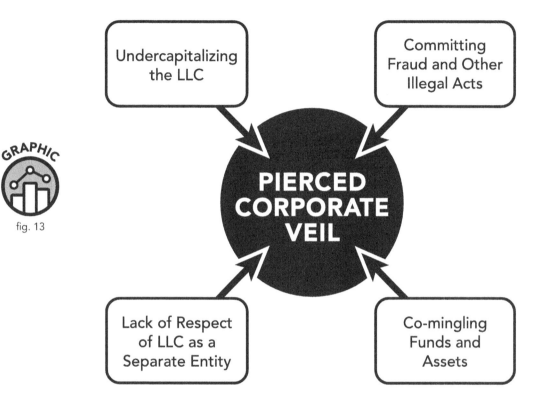

GRAPHIC

fig. 13

Examples of Piercing the Corporate Veil

On a more practical level, here are some examples of the practices previously described:

» **Undercapitalizing an LLC when it is formed**. Three friends got together and formed an LLC to package, sell, and deliver fresh produce to customers. They scarcely considered how much capital was necessary for this enterprise, and while contracting with growers to provide the produce they would need to supply their customers, they gave little thought to the costs of packaging, labor, fuel, and other expenses. At the same time, they misrepresented their worth to the growers, leading them to believe the company was well funded. They failed to tell the growers they could not pay them but continued to accept their produce, and ultimately the growers sued. The undercapitalization of the LLC and other factors prompted the court to rule in favor of the plaintiffs, piercing the LLC's corporate veil and leaving its members open to personal liability.

» **Commingling personal funds and assets with business funds and assets.** Josh started an LLC because he wanted to do residential construction and renovation work. He contracted with a customer to remake an attic into a bedroom suite, even though he didn't have enough money to purchase the materials he needed for the job. In the meantime, Josh was skimming money from his business account to pay the mortgage on his own house, which further limited his ability to conduct business or meet the terms of the contract he'd signed. These moves resulted in a court ruling in favor of piercing the veil, putting Josh's personal assets at risk.

» **Lack of respect on the part of the LLC's owner for the fact that the LLC is a separate entity.** Zimmerman leased private airplanes through his LLC. When he refused to pay an outstanding invoice for over $300,000 pursuant to these leases, the other party sued both Zimmerman and the LLC. After weighing several factors, the court decided to allow the other party to pierce the LLC's limited liability veil. Some of the important facts the court considered were as follows: a) Zimmerman frequently used leased private planes for personal travel; b) Zimmerman made several transfers between the private plane LLC and other companies he owned; c) he regularly withdrew funds from the LLC's operating bank account for his personal use; and d) the company no longer had assets because Zimmerman withdrew all the money before refusing to pay the invoice. This example is derived from a real-life case: *NetJets Aviation Inc. v. LHC Communications LLC*, 537 F.3d 168 (2nd Cir. 2008).

How to Avoid Piercing of the Veil

The most straightforward way to maintain your LLC's corporate veil is to play by the book when you form the company, pay close attention to your day-to-day operations, and make sure that each member is aware of the actions of other members.

Before you form the LLC, ensure that you have enough money to cover all the costs. If you can't make the necessary investment in the business, it's best to wait until you're able to save enough or obtain additional funds in some other way. This doesn't mean that you need thousands of dollars before pursuing your dream of owning your own business. You just need to have enough in reserve to maintain normal operations without allowing invoices to become overdue or relying on credit indefinitely.

As mentioned earlier, an operating agreement is put in place when an LLC is formed to spell out how things should be done and to make sure everyone agrees on how the business will be run. The agreement establishes the LLC as a separate entity that follows a set of rules and procedures. Sticking to the terms of your operating agreement is a big step in maintaining the LLC's corporate veil, which is something that every member should understand and adhere to. Make sure you keep the operating agreement up to date by making changes as applicable and conducting periodic reviews to assess the extent to which the agreement is being followed and whether any changes are needed. Also, keep records of company business that complies with the terms set out in your operating agreement, such as when you hold meetings or vote on issues. This makes it clear that you're respecting the business as a separate entity and upholding the terms of the operating agreement.

You know about the importance of maintaining separate business and personal financial accounts, and this cannot be stressed enough. Keeping those accounts separate is one of the most important things you can do to avoid having a court rule in favor of piercing the veil. If, for some reason, an individual must use business funds to cover a personal bill, that transaction should be documented as a loan or a draw, and proof exhibited when the money is repaid. On the flip side, if the business needs more money and an individual contributes personal funds, it should be documented as a capital contribution. Meanwhile, make sure all business expenses are documented and business accounts and credit cards kept separate from personal ones.

Practicing common sense is another important factor in maintaining your LLC's corporate veil. Follow all laws and regulations that pertain to your business, such as keeping up with state filings and paying all necessary taxes. Avoid any type of unlawful behavior, and don't hesitate to approach another LLC member if you know or even suspect that unlawful behavior is occurring. Maintaining good business practices at all times goes a long way toward keeping your LLC in compliance and its members protected.

I know this can seem overwhelming, but there is one overarching principle that, if you stick to it, will keep you out of trouble: treat your business like a business. If you view your business endeavor with the seriousness it requires and don't engage in acts you know are wrong, you will be fine.

Paying Attention to Licenses, Franchise Taxes, and Insurance

A big part of managing the day-to-day operations of a business is paying attention to matters such as licenses, taxes, and insurance, all of which can trip you up if you ignore them. Some business owners get impatient with having to spend time and energy on the details associated with keeping a business legal and in compliance, but not doing so can put your company at risk for fines, having to pay back taxes, and even having the business shut down. In this section we'll take a look at some tasks that can seem tedious but are really important to the success of your LLC. Let's start by considering the importance of getting the proper licenses and permits.

Getting the Proper Business Licenses and Permits

I've touched on business licenses and permits a few times in earlier chapters, but they're worth a closer look because it's likely that you need some sort of license to operate your business legally. You'll need to research which types of business licenses or permits are required in the state, county, and city in which your LLC is registered.

Even though LLCs are governed by the state in which they're registered and are not recognized on a federal level, certain business operations (figure 14) are regulated by federal agencies and require a federal license or permit.

If your LLC engages in any of these activities, you'll need to apply with the appropriate agency for a license or permit. Be prepared, as this could require that you provide a significant amount of information and that you conform to the agency's policies. Fees will vary by agency and business activity.

Most companies don't fall into one of the categories in figure 14 and won't require a federal license or permit, but your LLC is likely to need licenses or permits from the city, county, or state in which you operate. You're especially likely to need a state license if you run one of these businesses:

- » Childcare center
- » Dry cleaning shop
- » Electrical business
- » Hair and nail salon
- » Insurance agency
- » Mechanic shop
- » Plumbing business
- » Restaurant or food truck

GRAPHIC

fig. 14

TYPES OF BUSINESSES REGULATED BY A FEDERAL AGENCY	
AGRICULTURE	If your business imports or transports animals, animal products, biologics, biotechnology, or plants across state lines, you must have a license from the U.S. Department of Agriculture.
ALCOHOLIC BEVERAGES	If you manufacture, wholesale, or sell alcoholic beverages at a retail location, you'll need a license from the Alcohol and Tobacco Tax and Trade Bureau, as well as one from your local alcohol control board.
AVIATION	If your business includes operating some sort of aircraft, transporting people or goods by air, or maintenance of aircraft, you'll need a license from the Federal Aviation Administration.
FIREEARMS, AMMUNITION, & EXPLOSIVES	If your LLC manufactures, deals, or imports firearms, ammunitions, or explosives you must have a license from the Bureau of Alcohol, Tobacco, Firearms, and Explosives.
FISH & WILDLIFE	If your business involves any activity related to wildlife, including importing or exporting, you'll need a license from the U.S. Fish and Wildlife Service.
COMMERCIAL FISHERIES	If you engage in commercial fishing, you must get a license from the National Oceanic and Atmospheric Administration Fisheries Service.
MARITIME TRANSPORTATION	If your business provides ocean transportation or facilitates the shipment of cargo by sea, you must obtain a license from the Federal Maritime Commission.

MINING & DRILLING	If your LLC is involved in mining or drilling for natural gas, oil or other resources you'll need a license from the Bureau of Safety and Environmental Enforcement.
NUCLEAR ENERGY	If you produce commerical nuclear energy, distribute or dispose of nuclear materials, or operate a fuel cycle facility, you must have a license from the U.S. Nuclear Regulatory Commission.
RADIO & TV BROADCASTING	If your business broadcasts information by television, radio, wire, satellite, or cable, you'll need a license from the Federal Communications Commission.
TRANSPORTATION & LOGISTICS	If you operate an oversize or overweight vehicle, you should contact the U.S. Department of Transportation which will direct you to the agency in your state that can issue you a permit for oversize vehicles.

Don't assume, however, that you won't need a license or permit if your business is of a different type than those previously listed. In fact, it's best to assume you will need some type of license, even if it's not a general business license. You could need a license or permit to erect a sign at your business location, or a professional license if you work as an attorney, physician, accountant, therapist, or veterinarian. You might need a license to collect sales tax, or a permit to expand your building, or an emergency services permit.

Regardless of which licenses and permits you need, be sure you understand how long they're good for and that you must renew them in a timely manner to stay in compliance.

No matter what specific purpose they serve, business licenses and other permits are meant to regulate the types of businesses that operate in certain locations in order to protect public safety and health and to regulate land use. Having the appropriate licenses and/or permits signals to your customers that your business and professional status are legitimate. If you're not sure what licenses or permits you need, consult the US Small Business Administration to see whether you qualify as a small business for licensing purposes. Research what state licenses or permits are required by checking on your state's website, and check with your county and city offices to see if anything more is needed.

Franchise Taxes

Something else you'll want to keep close tabs on, if applicable, is *franchise taxes*. The name of this fee can be misleading, as one might mistakenly think it is a tax levied on a franchise of a company such as Great Clips or Dairy Queen. In this context, "franchise" refers to the limited liability protection granted by the state where the LLC is formed. A franchise tax is a tax imposed on certain businesses for their operation within certain states, even if they're not thought of as a franchise per se. Not every state has a franchise tax, but you'll need to know if yours does and pay the fee when it's due, if applicable.

Don't confuse this tax with federal or state income taxes; it must be paid in addition to those taxes. Franchise taxes are normally due every year or every other year, depending on the state, and they vary in how they're calculated. Some states calculate the tax based on a business's assets, while others charge a flat fee. That fee varies significantly from state to state. In California the franchise tax is $800 per year, and in Connecticut it's $80. In most states, the fee is about $100. Penalties for not paying the franchise tax vary from state to state, but most charge a late-payment fee.

About fourteen states have a franchise tax. The number has decreased over the past few years as certain states, such as Pennsylvania, Kansas, West Virginia, and Missouri, have voted to discontinue the tax in an effort to make themselves more business-friendly. Other states are seeking to do the same.

My home state of Texas requires franchise taxes to be paid only if the LLC brings in revenue over a certain threshold in one year, which, as of this writing in 2023, is $1,230,000. While no one likes to pay taxes, it's a good problem to have, because if you have to pay a franchise tax—in Texas at least—it means you own a million-dollar company. Compare that with Arkansas, which has a *minimum* annual franchise tax of $150, regardless of your LLC's annual income. You can see why entrepreneurs are flocking to the Lone Star State rather than the Natural State.

Having the Right Kinds of Insurance

Making sure you have the necessary types of insurance is another vital aspect of managing your business effectively. Even though your personal assets are separated from those of your LLC, there are many arguments to be made for gaining additional protection via business insurance. Depending on your situation, there are some types of insurance coverage you might want to consider to protect your business assets and put your mind at ease:

» **General liability insurance**. Liability insurance protects your LLC from situations like accidental property damage or injuries to other people. Remember the story in chapter 4 where Chris, a part-time employee of Jack's and Miguel's food truck business, backed into another food truck, damaging it enough to make it inoperable and resulting in repair costs and lost income? Fortunately, Jack and Miguel had purchased general liability insurance, which covered the cost of repairs to the food truck and its owner's lost income resulting from the accident.

» **Commercial property insurance**. If your LLC owns office equipment, furniture, inventory, or other property, commercial property insurance will pay to replace or repair it if it's damaged by something like a fire.

» **Business interruption insurance**. If a tree falls onto your office, smashing the roof and allowing rain to soak everything in the building, business interruption insurance can help keep you afloat until the space can be repaired and the contents replaced. Business interruption insurance may also cover expenses such as the cost of rent at a temporary location, employee salaries, and others.

The first three types of insurance mentioned here—general liability, commercial property, and business interruption insurance—are often sold bundled together under the category of "business owner policy." According to Insureon, an independent marketplace for online delivery of small-market insurance, the average cost of a business owner policy is about $57 a month.

» **Commercial auto insurance**. If you use your personal vehicle for work and coverage for business use isn't included in your personal policy, you may need commercial auto insurance.

» **Professional liability insurance**. Owners of professional LLCs can be held personally responsible for professional negligence—

commonly referred to as malpractice—even if they operate through a business entity, so it's important for them to protect themselves with professional liability insurance. This kind of insurance is also known as malpractice insurance or "errors and omissions" insurance.

» **Workers' compensation insurance**. Most states require workers' compensation insurance if a business has at least one employee. This type of insurance helps cover the costs of medical bills, lost wages, and other expenses if an employee is injured or becomes ill as a result of a workplace occurrence.

» **Product liability insurance**. If you manufacture, sell, or distribute a product, you might consider product liability insurance, which helps pay expenses if you're sued because your product causes injury or property damage. Civil liability for defective products extends across the supply chain. Retailers can be held liable for defective products even if their sole act was selling the product manufactured by a completely different company. Product liability insurance protects you from the negligence of others.

A business owner policy isn't terribly expensive, and it's a good place to start when assessing your insurance needs. You might begin with that and add other types of insurance as needed. Compare quotes from several insurance companies, either online or with an agent who specializes in small business insurance. You'll get the best rate if you mitigate risks to your LLC by instituting safety policies, installing alarms and making sure they work, reducing exposure to cybercrime, and taking other steps to safeguard your workplace.

Assessing Your LLC's Tax Situation

Because it's a question I often get from clients, I want to provide some information about changing the way your LLC is taxed. Regardless of how it's currently taxed, you can, under certain circumstances, change your LLC's tax status if it makes sense to do so.

Why might you want to change your LLC's tax status once it's up and running? Perhaps the membership has changed, and new members have different ideas about how the business should be taxed. Or it might be that some members' individual tax rates have increased, and it now makes sense to have your LLC classified as a corporation for tax purposes, to take advantage of the lower 21 percent flat tax rate a corporation pays.

Perhaps you've decided to apply for the special tax status of an S corp so you can qualify for the QBI (Qualified Business Income) deduction discussed in chapter 7. Or maybe you're tired of paying self-employment taxes, as a partnership must do, and want to be taxed as a C corp instead.

If you decide you want to change your tax status, you may be subject to the IRS's *60-month limitation rule*, a regulation that restricts an LLC from changing its tax status during the sixty months following its original decision about how to be taxed. There is an exception to this rule, however. If ownership of your LLC has changed by more than 50 percent since the decision was made regarding how it would be taxed, you can apply to the IRS for approval to change that election. There's no guarantee that the IRS will approve the change, but in the case of a shift in ownership, there's a good chance it will.

Jack and Miguel, owners of the One for the Road food truck company, had formed an LLC with Chris, their employee, and Angela and Haley as members. Each had equal ownership of the business, which they agreed should be taxed as a partnership. After three years, Chris received an offer to become a partner in a new restaurant that was starting up. He left the LLC, taking Angela and Haley with him. Fortunately, Jack and Miguel had been fielding inquiries from others who were interested in investing in their LLC, and they soon acquired four additional owners. These four new owners thought the business would be better off taxed as a corporation rather than as a partnership. Because more than half the ownership of the business had changed, they were not subject to the IRS's 60-month limitation rule and were able to change their LLC's tax status after only three years, or thirty-six months.

If you decide you want to change the way your LLC is taxed, just make sure it's for the right reason. And, unless there are special circumstances, be aware that you may be subject to the IRS's 60-month limitation rule.

LLC Expansion: Adding Members and Expanding to Other States

If your LLC is experiencing growth in terms of product, customers, capital, demand, and other measures, you might be considering how to expand your business. In this section, we'll examine two common methods of doing so: adding members and expanding your business to other states.

Neither of these methods is overly complicated, but you should have a thorough understanding of both the implications and the process of doing so before you move forward.

Adding Members to Your LLC

There are several reasons you may want to expand the membership of your LLC. Perhaps you need additional help or a person who has expertise in a particular area of business. You might add members who have cash to contribute to the business, or who have relationships that could be beneficial. For whatever reasons you choose to add members, do so thoughtfully, only expanding with people you're sure will benefit the business. Before you go ahead and vote on adding a new member, there are some things to consider:

No matter what a new member brings to the table, their presence decreases the percentage of profits that go to the current owners. Also, a new member represents an additional vote when it's time to make decisions regarding the business. If you're a single-member LLC, you'll now need to file taxes as a partnership or a corporation—you'll no longer have the option of filing as a sole proprietor. And finally, it may not be a simple process to remove a member from your LLC if things don't work out.

Nevertheless, LLCs add members all the time as they grow and maximize their business potential. To do so, you'll need to follow the terms of your operating agreement. If, for some reason, you don't have an operating agreement, or your agreement doesn't cover how new members will be added, you'll have to add those provisions to the agreement before adding any new members, or default to the laws governing LLCs in your state. If you add provisions to your operating agreement, members will need to vote on whether to accept them before you begin the process of adding another member. After consulting and following the guidelines in your LLC's operating agreement, be sure to check your state's laws to ascertain what documents you may need to file.

Single-member LLCs should also follow the guidelines laid out in their operating agreements, as well as any state laws that might apply. In some states, a single-member LLC has to dissolve and reconstitute in order to add additional members. If you are the owner of a single-member LLC, you must obtain an EIN (employer identification number) for your business if you don't already have one, and you will need to file Form 8832 to let the IRS know that you'll now be taxed as a partnership or a corporation.

Once you're clear about the terms of your operating agreement and/or your state's LLC laws, convene all members to discuss the implications and terms of adding a new member or members. You'll need to vote on whether to admit new members, so it's important that everyone agrees on things like what percentage of the business a new member will own and what percentage of profit or loss they're entitled to. When you've agreed on the terms, prepare an amendment to your operating agreement that lists the new owner's name, the capital contribution they're making, their percentage of ownership in the company, the percentage of profits or losses they'll receive, and any other pertinent information. Once that is completed, members can formally vote on whether to approve the amendment and admit the new member. Often, an LLC's operating agreement (and in some states, the law) requires a unanimous vote for admitting new members. Make sure to record the vote in meeting minutes and have all members sign the revised operating agreement.

Some states require LLCs to file an amendment to their articles of organization/certificate of formation when adding a member; check to see if that applies to you. While the logistics of adding a member to your LLC are fairly simple, be sure to consider the pros and cons carefully before doing so, because getting rid of a member could turn out to be messier and more complicated than adding one.

Expanding Your LLC to Other States

In chapter 3, I discuss establishing your LLC in a state other than the one in which you live, and I'd like to go into a little more detail about that here. Most LLC owners I work with are content with a single-location business, but there are some great reasons to expand your business across state lines, including accessing new markets and increasing your revenues and profits. However, establishing a foreign LLC, requires planning and careful execution, so think it over carefully before starting the process.

It should be noted that a **_foreign LLC_** isn't an LLC formed in a different country. Rather, it is an LLC formed under the laws of a different state. My clients regularly get confused about this. The term is essentially uniform across the country, so remember that it might apply to you despite the word "foreign" being included.

The first thing to consider if you're thinking about expanding your business to another state is whether you really need to do so. In most cases, you don't need to register as a foreign LLC if you're simply selling products and services to customers there. You're generally only required to register as a foreign LLC if you have a physical store or a manufacturing or distribution facility there, or if you've hired salespeople or distributors to sell your product there. You may be required to register in another state if you open a bank account or buy business property there, or if you conduct business meetings with clients or customers there or have employees who live there. Requirements vary from state to state, so if your LLC is involved in a state other than where you formed the business, spend some time researching its laws to figure out if you need to register there. A good place to start is the secretary of state's website for the state in question.

If you are required to register as a foreign LLC in a particular state and you don't do so, you could face some pretty serious consequences, including having to pay fines and interest for the time your LLC was doing business in that state and wasn't registered. You might also have to deal with payment of back taxes and the filing fees you should have paid to that state. Also, your personal assets could be at risk because a court could rule that your failure to observe state law warrants allowing a future litigant to pierce your LLC's corporate veil. If you think you might do business in another state, take the necessary steps to get registered there if you need to.

Some of those steps overlap with what you have to do when you first form your LLC. Requirements for registering as a foreign LLC are similar in most states, but always start with the secretary of state (or equivalent position) to confirm what you'll need to do. Generally, you'll need to take the following steps to qualify as a foreign LLC:

» Submit a ***Certificate of Authority***, which is a form that shows you're authorized to do business in a state other than your formation state. As with several other forms discussed in this book, the name of this form varies—Application for Registration, Qualification Certificate, and others are used.

» Conduct a business name search to make sure your LLC's name is legally available in the state in question. If it is not, you'll need to use a fictitious name in that state.

» Designate a registered agent in the new state. States often have listings of authorized registered agents on their websites, or you could find an online company that has agents with the authority to act anywhere in the United States.

» Obtain the necessary licenses and permits. These will vary depending on the state, so be sure you take time to find out what you'll need. It's especially important to clarify whether you'll have to collect sales tax in the state. In some states, just having an employee there is enough to require that sales tax be collected and remitted to the state's revenue department. In that case, you'll have to apply for a sales tax permit.

» Register for payroll taxes if you have employees in the new state. You'll need to get a state income tax withholding number and an unemployment insurance number and withhold state income taxes from employees' pay. If there's no state income tax (Alaska, Florida, Nevada, New Hampshire, South Dakota, Tennessee, Texas, Washington, and Wyoming), you'll still be required to withhold and pay federal income tax. Plus, you'll have to register with the state's Department of Labor and follow guidelines concerning minimum wage, workers' compensation, state disability insurance, and any labor laws.

If you expand your LLC from the state in which it was formed, you'll need to keep up with all the requirements of every state in which it's registered, making sure you have all the necessary types of insurance, that you keep your permits and licenses updated, that you file annual reports, and so forth. Pay special attention to the tax codes of the new state(s); you must understand your tax obligations as a foreign entity. There are a lot of moving parts when it comes to expanding your business to another state, but many of the steps you'll take are not all that different from what you did when you formed your LLC originally. Consult your business plan, consider the steps carefully, and cover all your bases.

Chapter Recap

» Certain things must be done to make sure your LLC remains in compliance with the law. These include filing reports, maintaining the necessary licenses and permits, keeping your insurance policies up to date, and paying franchise taxes, if applicable.

» There are instances in which it makes sense to change the way your LLC is taxed—for example, when you elect to be taxed as a corporation to avoid self-employment taxes or as an S corp to qualify for the QBI deduction.

» Adding members to your LLC can be advantageous but is not something that should be done without forethought and planning.

» There is a series of steps you'll need to take to register your LLC as a foreign entity in a state other than the one in which it was originally formed.

| 10 |

Dissolving Your LLC

Chapter Overview
- » The Business Life Cycle
- » Dissolving an LLC
- » Selling an LLC

It may seem strange to include a chapter about dissolving your LLC in a book that's otherwise all about getting it started and overseeing the day-to-day operations, but if at some point you decide it's time to let the business go, it's important to understand how that should happen. If a dissolution is not carried out properly, the LLC's members could face tax consequences or become personally liable to the LLC's remaining creditors.

There are a number of reasons an LLC might need to be dissolved, some of which we'll discuss in this chapter. The need to close a business can result from unforeseen personal circumstances, poor business decisions, legal or tax problems, and a variety of other reasons. Some LLCs are formed with a specific timeline in place from the start, with the understanding that the LLC will be dissolved at a certain time. Other LLCs are formed to address a particular need and are dissolved when that need has been filled. Sometimes they are voluntarily dissolved and in other circumstances are dissolved by the state or a judge. This chapter walks you through the various types of dissolutions and the steps required to formally close a business.

Something I'd like to make clear up front is that dissolving a business doesn't mean that you've failed. Entrepreneurs close businesses all the time, for a host of reasons, only to regroup and open another one. Let's get started by exploring that idea a little more closely.

Failure is simply the opportunity to begin again, this time more intelligently.
– HENRY FORD

Closing a Business Doesn't Mean You Failed

As we all know, businesses come and go. You can probably think of a location in your neighborhood that has housed four or five different businesses over the past ten or fifteen years, or a business that opened with great fanfare, only to be shuttered a year and a half later. Business partners have a falling-out and agree they can no longer work together, or owners realize they don't have the capitalization they need to stay open. The company might have been opened in a terrible location or have been dependent on a couple of key customers who took their business elsewhere.

The chances of these scenarios happening can be lessened if you have a good business plan, which I discuss in the first chapter of this book. But events that can't be anticipated sometimes occur, and businesses must close. If you follow the plan outlined in the earlier chapters of this book, take the time to complete all the steps that are necessary to get an LLC up and running, and keep on top of what must be done to stay in compliance, I'm betting on the success of your business. But if, for some reason, it doesn't succeed and you're forced to dissolve it, don't assume your days as an entrepreneur are over. I've seen many people close a business only to start a better one a few years later.

Even if your enterprise is currently thriving, be aware that there is general agreement among experts that most businesses experience a four-stage life cycle. What these stages are called varies, but they're often referred to as Introduction, Growth, Maturity, and Decline (figure 15).

BUSINESS LIFE CYCLE

fig. 15

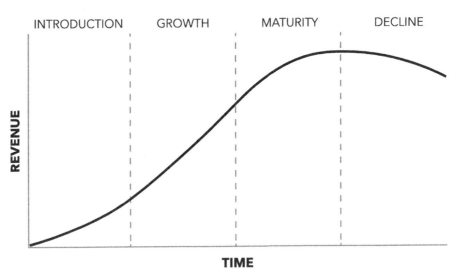

There are plenty of books about business life cycles, and we're not going to go into detail about it here. Suffice it to say that each stage involves challenges and opportunities. There's no prescribed timeline for the stages of a business life cycle; some of the stages can extend over many years. But in most cases, for whatever reasons, businesses will eventually reach an end point and dissolve.

Bed Bath & Beyond, a big-box staple in many communities for decades, announced in April 2023 it had filed for bankruptcy protection and would be closing all its stores in the coming months. There were a lot of reasons for the company's demise, but experts cited a failure to deal with the fierce competition presented by online shopping, along with an unstable management structure.

The decision to dissolve an LLC can be a difficult one, but sometimes it is necessary. If you are ever in the position of having to dissolve a business, know that the process should be systematically conducted, without leaving any loose ends that could cause problems down the road. Let's start by considering the ways an LLC can be dissolved.

Types of Dissolutions

Common classifications for LLC dissolutions are voluntary dissolution, judicial dissolution, administrative dissolution, tax termination, and loss of license to practice. Let's take a closer look at each of them.

Voluntary Dissolution

An LLC can be voluntarily dissolved by its members at any time after formation. Some voluntary dissolutions are planned, and others are not. Members may have agreed to dissolve the LLC on a specific date or following the occurrence of a certain event, as laid out in the LLC's operating agreement. The death of a member, for instance, could trigger a *voluntary dissolution*. Some LLCs are formed for a limited purpose, such as to fund and film a movie or to buy and flip a house, with the understanding that when the purpose has been fulfilled—the movie released, the house sold—the LLC will be dissolved.

An LLC can dissolve because members disagree on a major issue and have reached an impasse, or because the business is no longer economically feasible. If all members agree to a voluntary dissolution, it is a relatively simple process. As long as there are no legal issues pending, you simply perform certain tasks and file ***articles of dissolution***, the opposite of articles of incorporation, with the secretary of state.

Judicial Dissolution

Usually a less happy affair than a voluntary dissolution, a ***judicial dissolution*** is a legal process in which a court dissolves a business. These types of closures don't happen often, but when they do, it's typically because of something like fraud, mismanagement, or breach of fiduciary duty. A judicial dissolution is usually initiated by a state attorney general, an unsatisfied creditor, or one or more LLC members. A court then reviews the case and decides whether to dissolve the LLC.

Administrative Dissolution

This type of dissolution is mentioned in chapter 9 as part of a discussion about the importance of filing necessary reports. Failure to do so can result in an administrative dissolution, which is when the state steps in and shuts a business down.

If you're ever facing an administrative dissolution, you have a good chance of fixing the problem by quickly filing any missed reports, catching up on unpaid taxes, and handing over a penalty payment to the state (all this depends on which state your LLC was formed in). Once this is done, the state can reinstate your business. But if you don't address a notice of administrative dissolution, the state can permanently dissolve the LLC.

Loss of License to Practice

If you have a PLLC (professional LLC) and you lose your license to practice, you'll have to dissolve the business. The reason why your license was pulled doesn't matter. Continuing to perform licensed business when you no longer have a license is an easy way to end up in prison.

How to Dissolve an LLC

If you've decided to dissolve your LLC, there are certain steps needed to begin the proceedings and keep them moving forward. Hopefully, your operating agreement establishes when and how the LLC will be dissolved. If it doesn't, follow the default laws of your state's LLC act.

I hope one of your major takeaways from this book is the importance of a well-thought-out and well-executed operating agreement for your LLC. Because LLCs enjoy such flexibility, you can craft your operating agreement to steer your business in the direction that works best for all partners. If you don't do that, you're forced to follow state regulations, which may not be the most advantageous for your LLC.

If the dissolution is a voluntary one, members will need to vote on the matter unless your operating agreement contains guidelines for dissolution in the case of a specific event, such as the death of a partner.

Generally, closing down your business involves three steps: dissolution, winding up of affairs, and termination of the LLC (figure 16).

3 STEPS TO CLOSING YOUR LLC

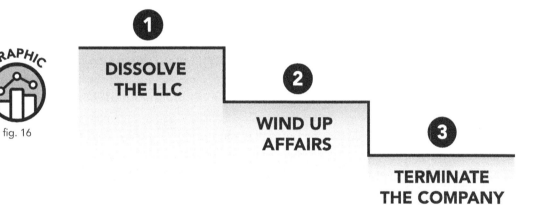

GRAPHIC

fig. 16

1
DISSOLVE THE LLC

2
WIND UP AFFAIRS

3
TERMINATE THE COMPANY

Dissolving the LLC

These steps might seem puzzling because the distinction between dissolution and termination can be tricky to understand. Dissolving your LLC is not the same as terminating its existence. When the LLC is dissolved, it doesn't shut down completely. Dissolution means that it will no longer conduct business; it still exists, but only for the purpose of winding up affairs and shutting down.

Dissolution of an LLC begins with a *triggering event*, which is any occurrence that requires the business to cease operations and prepare for termination. The triggering event may or may not be stipulated in the operating agreement.

If the LLC was formed for the purpose of flipping a house, for instance, the triggering event would be the sale of the house, if that was stipulated in the operating agreement. If there's no named event that results in the dissolution of the LLC, then the triggering event is likely to be a vote by the members.

Review your operating agreement and see what provisions apply to voting to dissolve the LLC. Your agreement might specify what percentage or number of members must approve the dissolution (and it might deal with other formalities). If your operating agreement doesn't address voting on dissolution, you'll abide by your state's laws pertaining to LLCs. Some states require a unanimous vote for dissolution, and others stipulate a simple majority.

When you hold your vote, be sure to cover all the bases by carefully documenting everything that pertains to it. You'll want to hold a formal meeting, record minutes, and have a formal document for members to sign once the vote is taken. Documenting everything carefully as the proceedings occur prevents situations like someone coming back in the future and claiming they were excluded from or misinformed about the vote.

Many states require that you file a document called *articles of dissolution* after the LLC has been dissolved. It includes the name of the LLC, when it was formed and when it was dissolved, and the event that triggered the dissolution. Filing the document signals that the LLC must cease its regular business and begin the process of winding up its affairs.

Winding Up Affairs

The winding-up stage is when the assets of your LLC are liquidated and distributed and a host of other matters are attended to. Normally, the first step of winding up is to settle all your debts and pay your creditors. How you do this depends on the regulations of your state, so be sure to fully understand them before moving ahead.

Your LLC's liability protection is likely to weaken upon dissolution, meaning you should be as careful as possible when dealing with creditors, debts, and claims. Keep meticulous records and document all your actions.

In this context, any unpaid debt or existing liability — such as unpaid utility bills or payroll for your employees — are referred to as a *claim*.

During the process of satisfying debts and creditors, you might encounter claims, which are actions brought against a company. These could be known claims or unknown claims. **Known claims**, just as you'd think, are those the owners of the LLC know about. **Unknown claims**, you guessed it, are claims of which the LLC's owners are unaware. For example, if the LLC failed to pay its workers overtime as required by federal and state law because the law changed during the company's lifetime, that liability would be an unknown claim. Your state laws lay out how creditors must be handled, the order in which they are to be paid, and how you must deal with known and unknown claims. Normally, a notification letter is sent to every known creditor, stating that the business is closing and specifying the date it will close, the deadline for the creditor to submit any invoices to the business (typically they are given at least 120 days), and the address to which the invoices should be sent. Be sure to send these letters by certified mail or through a tracked parcel delivery service such as FedEx so you have a record of each one.

If a creditor doesn't respond within the specified time, their claim is no longer valid, and you won't have to pay the invoice. Also, you have the option of rejecting a claim if you don't think it's valid. If you accept a claim, you can try to negotiate with the creditor to pay a lesser amount.

To deal with unknown claims, which could result from things such as a faulty product or negligence on the part of an LLC member, you need to file a public notice of the dissolution of your LLC. How it's filed can vary from state to state, but usually the notice is filed in a local newspaper. In it, you state that your LLC is closing, and you specify a deadline by which to receive any claims to be filed against it. You should also include a mailing address where claims should be sent and what information they must include. If you're registered in more than one state, you'll have to file the dissolution notice in each one. If you're worried that your LLC could have significant liabilities from unknown creditors, you can get insurance to cover some or all of the claims, or self-insure by setting money aside for this purpose before it's distributed to members.

Once creditors have been notified, close out any bank accounts that don't need to be kept open for bill payments. Cancel all business licenses, permits, and assumed names; pay any taxes owed, file final tax returns and reports, and formally withdraw from any states where you were registered as a foreign LLC. All these tasks must be completed before the LLC can be terminated. In the next section is a complete checklist of what's involved in closing down a business.

The final step in the winding up of affairs is to distribute any remaining assets among members. Hopefully your operating agreement specifies how that should be done. In case it doesn't, the Internal Revenue Code of the IRS states the order in which members should be paid. It typically looks something like this:

» Members who are owed distributions or have made loans to the company must be paid back before other members receive any funds.

» The initial contribution of each member gets paid back next. This can get tricky if there isn't enough money remaining to pay everyone back. If that's the case, the remaining funds would likely be split in proportion to the amount of the initial contributions. But that could vary depending on your state laws and your operating agreement.

» Any remaining money is normally distributed to members in accordance with their percentage of ownership. Someone who owns 20 percent of the business, for instance, would get 20 percent of whatever cash is left over. It doesn't have to be done that way, but that's the simplest method. If you want to operate differently, you'll need to create a formal resolution that shows all members in agreement with it.

Terminating the LLC

Once you've taken care of everything involved with closing your business, the LLC is considered terminated. You might have to file one more document, depending on your state. This document states that all debt and liability have been satisfied and any remaining assets distributed. It's known as articles of termination or **_articles of cancellation_**.

Closing an LLC can seem complicated, and there are many steps you must take to do it the right way. But don't be tempted to simply shutter the business and walk away; doing so still leaves you responsible for taxes, annual reports, and other obligations, which, if not met, can result in legal problems. Also, business thieves are known to be on the lookout for companies listed on state records as delinquent or administratively dissolved, and they take advantage of them by stealing their identities and applying for loans or other types of assets in their names.

No matter the reasons you have terminated your LLC, once the process is complete, take some time to think about everything you learned and all the experience you gained. If you decide you want to get back in business, there could be a way to reactivate the LLC. The rules for doing this vary from state to state and can be complicated. An easier way to proceed would probably be to open a new business, using the name of your previous LLC or starting fresh with a new name.

Steps in Closing Down an LLC

It's likely that your LLC's operating agreement contains information about the circumstances under which the LLC should be dissolved and how a dissolution should be handled. Consult your operating agreement before making decisions regarding the closing of a business. If your operating agreement doesn't establish when and how the LLC will be terminated, you'll need to follow the default laws of your state's LLC act.

1. Dissolve the LLC. This can occur through a triggering event or a vote by members. If a vote occurs, be sure to carefully document everything pertaining to it.

2. File articles of dissolution with your state, if required.

3. Settle all debts and pay all creditors.

4. Close any bank accounts that won't be needed for payment of bills.

5. Cancel all business licenses, registrations, permits, insurance policies, and assumed names.

6. Pay any taxes that are owed, and file final tax returns and reports.

7. Formally withdraw from any states in which the LLC was registered as a foreign LLC.

8. Distribute any remaining assets among members.

9. File articles of termination with your state, if required.

10. Maintain all records pertaining to the closing.

Selling Your LLC

Selling a business is different from dissolving it. Selling your LLC means you transfer its ownership to another person or group of people; dissolving it means you simply close it down. As with dissolving an LLC, rules pertaining to selling one vary from state to state, so be sure to find out what your state requires. Still, there are some general guidelines to follow no matter where you're located.

If you plan to sell your company, you'll need to know what it is worth. This can be difficult, as it's hard not to let sentiment cloud your judgment of the business's actual value. If necessary, you can hire a small business appraiser to conduct a valuation.

You'll need a full account of the business's debts, including bank loans, outstanding vendor bills, and rent or mortgage costs. You'll also need to gather all documents related to your LLC's financial and business operations, including articles of organization, operating agreement, and any certifications that show the business is in good standing with the state. Have available several years of business tax returns, building and equipment leases, customer and vendor contracts, profit and loss statements, and accounts receivable and payable reports.

To locate potential buyers, consider posting notices on business sale websites such as BizQuest, BizBuySell, or BusinessesForSale.com, or buy ad space in a local business journal or trade publication. Don't rule out the possibility that a competitor may be interested in purchasing your business; reach out to them if you're considering that option. Another possibility is hiring a ***business broker***, which is an individual or company that can help you locate a buyer, secure a good price, submit paperwork, deal with licensing and permits, and perform other tasks related to selling a business.

Once you've located a buyer, you'll need to negotiate the terms of the sale. This will vary dramatically depending on the type of business you have and other circumstances, but you'll want to consider factors such as whether you want to sell the entire business entity or just its client list or its business assets. You'll also want to determine whether the buyer will pay a lump sum or give you a down payment with installments to follow.

If you are a single-member LLC, selling your business is normally a straightforward process, since you get to make the decisions on your own. With a multimember LLC, all members need to approve the terms of the sale. Hopefully your operating agreement contains specifications for selling the business, and you can follow those instructions carefully. Once the business has been sold, the articles of organization, operating agreement, and any supplemental documents should be changed to reflect the new ownership.

When the sale has been completed, simply divide the proceeds between members and consider your next steps. When starting an LLC or any type of business, it's smart to have an end plan in mind, whether it's running the business for a specified period of time and then cashing out, expanding to other states, or another strategy. However, we know that life doesn't always happen as planned, and there are instances in which a business is forced to be sold or dissolved on short notice. It's well worth the effort to take some time to consider how you would handle that scenario.

Steps in Selling an LLC

Regulations regarding selling a business vary from state to state, so be aware of the rules that apply to you before beginning the process. Here are seven steps you must take to sell your LLC:

1. Determine the actual value of the LLC.

2. Gather and organize all documents related to your LLC's financial and business operations.

3. Notify potential buyers that the business is for sale.

4. Negotiate the terms of the sale once a buyer has been located.

5. Have all members vote to approve the terms of the sale.

6. Change the articles of organization, the operating agreement, and any supplemental documents to reflect the new ownership.

7. Divide the proceeds of the sale between LLC members.

Chapter Recap

» Many business experts adhere to the theory of a business life cycle, which includes four phases: introduction, growth, maturity, and decline.

» There are several types of dissolution for an LLC, including voluntary, judicial, administrative, tax termination, and dissolution as a result of loss of license to practice.

» Specific steps must be taken to shut down an LLC: dissolving the LLC, winding up affairs, and terminating the business.

» Selling an LLC is different from dissolving it and can be a valuable part of a long-term business plan.

Conclusion

Getting a business off the ground is a significant accomplishment, so if you've already made that leap and have your LLC up and running, I offer my congratulations! For those who are still contemplating that move, I offer my encouragement and support. The American economy only thrives when hardworking people such as yourselves decide they have something unique to offer through entrepreneurship. Each of you has something special to offer and I am overjoyed that you have decided to begin your journey.

While I'm confident this book provides all the information you need to form an LLC and keep it in compliance with regulators as you manage the day-to-day operations of the business, I would urge you to continue reading and learning as you gain experience as an entrepreneur. Economic conditions impact businesses, operations tend to get a little more complicated as your business grows, and regulations can change, so it's best to stay in the know. All education is self-education, and it never ends.

Speaking of how regulations change, almost every business in America—including LLCs—have a new federal reporting requirement in 2024 pursuant to the Corporate Transparency Act. The Financial Crimes Enforcement Network (FinCEN), a bureau of the U.S. Department of Treasury, now requires any business formed by registering with its state's Secretary of State or similar office to report their beneficial ownership information (BOI)— name, address, Social Security number, and other biographical information—for anyone who controls the business or owns over 25% of its equity. The purpose of the report is intended to make it harder for people to form shell companies or similar entities to use for illegal activity, such as money laundering or drug trafficking. Reports are due by Jan. 1, 2025, for existing companies and within 90 days of formation for new companies. If you're not familiar with this new requirement and want to find out if you'll be required to file the necessary information, you can read all about it on FinCEN's website at fincen.gov/boi. I have also included a guide for this new law as a Digital Asset for this book.

I've offered this example of a regulation change to make a point about the importance of seeking out information that keeps you up to date on issues related to businesses. There are plenty of resources available, some of which are listed in Appendix I of this book and included with the Digital Assets on the book's website. The more you learn, the better equipped you'll be to run your business. I especially urge you to pay attention to tax issues, environmental regulations, insurance requirements, and other areas of regulation that tend to change more often than others.

Staying informed enables you to act with confidence because you have the knowledge you need to make informed and smart decisions. Perhaps at some point you'll want to expand your business to operate in additional states, take on some partners, or change the way that your company is taxed. Knowing what to expect and what will be required in any of those situations helps you to be better prepared to move forward.

One thing is for certain: There is no shortage of information available. As such, I'd urge you to be discerning when choosing your learning resources, to make sure you employ reputable sources of information. If you're lucky enough to have a business mentor you can count on for advice and information, you're ahead of the game. If you don't have a mentor, you might consider joining a local business organization such as a Chamber of Commerce to make connections and meet people you can learn from.

As you move forward with your business, whatever that business looks like, try to remain optimistic, open to new ideas, and be willing to pivot when necessary. There will be good days and bad days, so just keep moving forward, one step at a time. In the words of Steve Chou, a hugely successful businessperson and author of *The Family First Entrepreneur*, keep in mind "the most entrepreneurial trait there is: the ability to persist."

REMEMBER TO DOWNLOAD
YOUR FREE DIGITAL ASSETS!

 **Sample Operating Agreement**

 **State-by-State LLC Formation Guide**

 **Business Plan Template**

 **LLC Formation Checklist**

TWO WAYS TO ACCESS YOUR FREE DIGITAL ASSETS

Use the camera app on your mobile phone to scan the QR code
or visit the link below and instantly access your digital assets.

or

go.quickstartguides.com/llc

SCAN ME

VISIT URL

Appendix I

Additional Resources

In addition to this book, there are many other resources that may be useful to you. Updated information may be released following the publication of this book, but these books, web resources, and podcasts can help you get started.

Books

» *Accounting for Non-Accountants: Financial Accounting Made Simple for Beginners* by Wayne Label

» *Accounting QuickStart Guide: The Simplified Beginner's Guide to Real-World Financial and Managerial Accounting for Students, Business Owners, and Finance Professionals* by Josh Bauerle

» *Agency, Partnership, and the LLC in a Nutshell* by J. Dennis Hynes and Mark Loewenstein

» *Running & Growing a Business QuickStart Guide: The Simplified Beginner's Guide to Becoming an Effective Leader, Developing Scalable Systems, and Growing Your Business Profitably* by Ken Colwell, PhD, MBA

» *Starting a Business QuickStart Guide: The Simplified Beginner's Guide to Launching a Successful Small Business, Turning Your Vision into Reality, and Achieving Your Entrepreneurial Dream* by Ken Colwell, PhD, MBA

» *The Complete Book of Business Plans: Simple Steps to Writing Powerful Business Plans* by Brian Hazelgren and Joseph A. Covello

» *The Harvard Business Review Entrepreneur's Handbook: Everything You Need to Launch and Grow Your New Business* by Harvard Business Review

Web Resources

Starting and running a business are challenging tasks. There's a lot to learn and undertake, but web resources that offer tools such as accounting software, educational resources, or a community of other business owners who can support you can be useful tools to help you move forward.

Here are some web resource recommendations from Mashable, PC Magazine, Forbes, Investopedia, and Cybernews.

Website builders for small businesses:

» **Wix**. One of the most popular website builders available, Wix, provides cloud-based web development services and enables users to create HTML5 websites and mobile sites using online drag-and-drop tools. It offers three types of editors, thousands of plugins, and hundreds of themes. Wix offers a free starting plan, or you can get a paid subscription with enhanced features and no ads.

» **Hostinger**. Another drag-and-drop website builder, Hostinger, lets you start building from scratch, pick from more than a hundred designer-made templates, or have AI build a website for you. The site is said to offer an excellent user interface and some unique and powerful tools that let you control the look and functions of your online presence. Low-price plans are available, or you can upgrade as needed.

» **Squarespace**. This site can help you create a customizable website or online store and offers free, unlimited hosting. It features integrated safety features, flexible templates, and drag-and-drop elements that let you build a site quickly, without the need for any coding. You can get a free trial and then pay for a business plan starting at $23 a month.

Accounting software for small businesses:

» **QuickBooks Online**. The choice of many small business accounting professionals, QuickBooks offers an array of online training resources and forums for support, as needed. It helps you track income and expenses, accept credit card and ACH payments, and learn more about growing your business. The program is cloud-based and has a mobile app. It integrates with hundreds of apps such as TurboTax, PayPal, Amazon, Shopify, and others. It offers four plans to accommodate a range of users.

» **Zoho Books.** Easy to use and cloud-based, Zoho Books offers an invoice, inventory, and project management system. It has a free plan, or you can invest in a premium plan for additional features. The program sends customizable invoices and connects to payment gateways that allow customers to pay you online. The dashboard lets you easily view your biggest expenses, total receivables, payables, and sales, and you can create a variety of business reports, including balance sheets and cash flow statements.

» **FreshBooks.** Designed for single-member LLCs, freelancers, and sole proprietors, FreshBooks allows you to quickly draft invoices; keep track of payments owed; and accept payment through credit and debit cards, ACH, Stripe, and PayPal. You can get a free trial and a variety of plans starting at $15 a month.

Podcasts

One thing you're sure to realize as a business owner is that you never stop learning—and that's a good thing. Keeping your mind open to new ideas and new ways of doing things helps you be creative, innovative, and resourceful.

Podcasts, most of which can be downloaded for free, have become a popular learning medium, with a multitude of topics available to entertain, inspire, and teach. And you can listen to them while you're at the gym, taking a walk, or driving to meet with a customer or supplier, thus keeping yourself up to date and well informed about interesting topics. Here are some podcasts that are recommended for small business owners.

» **Marketplace.** Aired on public radio stations across the country, each episode of Marketplace is also published on the web. The show, hosted by Kai Ryssdal, can keep you up to date with current economic news. It's extremely user-friendly, delivering complex topics in an understandable and entertaining manner.

» **Entrepreneurs on Fire.** With more than 3000 episodes, this award-winning podcast is sure to offer something of interest to everyone. Founded and hosted by John Lee Dumas, the podcast features interviews with leading entrepreneurs who offer inspiring stories about their careers, share advice, and educate their listeners.

» **How I Built This**. This podcast, hosted by Guy Raz, is a fascinating look at how the world's best-known entrepreneurs started their businesses and built iconic brands like Harry's Razors, Tory Burch, Ben & Jerry's, and Orangetheory Fitness. An excellent interviewer, Raz gets his guests to talk about their mistakes, doubts, and triumphs. The episodes are interesting and encouraging to entrepreneurs at any level.

» **Duct Tape Marketing**. If you don't know much about marketing your business, this podcast provides valuable information about how to reach more potential customers without spending a lot of money. It's hosted by John Jantsch, a small business marketing speaker and consultant, and the episodes cover a wide range of marketing-related content.

» **School of Greatness**. Host Lewis Howes covers a wide range of topics in the episodes of this podcast, all with the theme of how to reach greatness in your life. Episodes include lifestyle advice and tips for achieving wealth, being successful in business, and ensuring that your business thrives. School of Greatness is one of the top-ranked business and self-development podcasts on iTunes.

Appendix II

Summary of Important Tax Forms

Filing the right tax forms, and on time, is an important part of keeping your LLC compliant with the law. For that reason, I've included a list of tax forms that are important for LLCs. Which ones you need to file depends on the circumstances of your LLC, so be sure to fully understand how your LLC is taxed. You may also need to file forms not listed here. You can find out exactly which forms your LLC should file, and how you should file, on the "Tax Information for Businesses" page of the IRS website at www.irs.gov/businesses.

Before you start thinking about the tax forms you'll need to file, remember that you first have to obtain an Employer Identification Number (EIN), because the IRS requires you to have that in order to file your taxes. You can apply for your EIN online, using IRS Form SS-4.

» All LLCs must file an IRS Form 8832, commonly referred to as the "check the box" form. This enables you to inform the IRS of how you elect your LLC to be taxed.

» A single-member LLC should file IRS Form 1040, Schedule C. With a single-member LLC, your taxes are based on your personal income rate.

» A multimember LLC will file IRS Form 1065, US Return of Partnership Income, and each member must file a Schedule K-1 that indicates their share of partnership income, credits, and deductions.

» If the LLC is a corporation, normal corporate tax rules will apply to the LLC and it should file an IRS Form 1120, US Corporation Income Tax Return.

» If the LLC elected to be taxed as an S corp, it should file an IRS Form 1120-S, US Income Tax Return for an S-Corporation. Each member must report their share of corporate income, credits, and deductions on Schedule K-1.

» If your LLC has employees, you'll file IRS Form 940, the Employer's Annual Federal Unemployment Tax Return. You'll also need to file either IRS Form 941, the Employer's Quarterly Federal Tax Return, or IRS Form 944, the Employer's Annual Federal Tax Return.

About the Author

MATTHEW C. LEWIS, ESQ.

Matthew C. Lewis developed an interest in the law and legal systems at an early age. He graduated *magna cum laude* from the University of Texas in Arlington with a bachelor of arts in criminology before pursuing a law degree. He graduated *summa cum laude* from the University of Arkansas in Little Rock's William H. Bowen School of Law, where he served as an associate editor of the UALR Law Review.

Born and raised in Texarkana, Texas, a city located near the border of Arkansas, Matthew is well versed in both Texas and Arkansas law and serves clients in those and other states. A firm believer that legal services should be available to all who need them, he regularly works with legal nonprofits to provide reduced cost or pro bono services to those in need of them. He strives to provide high-quality legal services at affordable prices that are affordable for those who need them by leveraging technological advances in telecommunications and digital libraries and employing innovative billing solutions.

Matthew has helped many clients start businesses, remain in compliance with laws and regulations, and sell or close down those businesses at the appropriate time. He serves as legal counsel for a number of businesses and has a thorough understanding of the challenges and daily demands business owners encounter. An appreciation of the financial constraints many owners of small businesses face was a major impetus in his decision to write this book, which he believes can serve as an instruction manual for how to start an LLC.

His wish is that readers will benefit from the advice this book offers and experience success in starting and operating their businesses.

About QuickStart Guides

QuickStart Guides are books for beginners, written by experts.

QuickStart Guides® are comprehensive learning companions tailored for the beginner experience. Our books are written by experts, subject matter authorities, and thought leaders within their respective areas of study.

For nearly a decade more than 850,000 readers have trusted QuickStart Guides® to help them get a handle on their finances, start their own business, invest in the stock market, find a new hobby, get a new job—the list is virtually endless.

The QuickStart Guides® series of books is published by ClydeBank Media, an independent publisher based in Albany, NY.

Connect with QuickStart Guides online at www.quickstartguides.com or follow us on Facebook, Instagram, and LinkedIn.

Follow us @quickstartguides

Glossary

60-month limitation rule
A regulation that, with exceptions, prevents an LLC from changing the manner in which it is taxed within 60 months of the original decision regarding its taxation.

Accrual accounting
An accounting system that records revenue when a product or service is delivered to a customer, rather than when payment for the service or product is received.

Adjusted gross income
Total gross income minus specific deductions permitted by the IRS.

Administrative dissolution
An action a state can take to rescind your LLC's ability to do business.

Annual report
A report on your LLC's activities that must be filed periodically with the state in which your LLC is registered.

Arbitration
A private trial overseen by an arbitrator instead of a judge that enables members of an LLC to resolve disputes without taking the matter to court.

Articles of dissolution
A document that many states require after an LLC has been dissolved.

Articles of Organization
A public document containing basic information relevant to the business that an LLC must file in the state where it will be based.

Assignment of contract
An agreement allowing one party to transfer the rights and benefits of a contract to another party. It is commonly used when converting a sole proprietorship or general partnership to an LLC.

Business broker
An individual or company that specializes in locating buyers and providing other services for clients who are looking to sell a business.

C-corporation
Also known as a C-corp, referring to any corporation that is taxed separately from its owners and has not been designated as an S-corp.

Cash-based accounting
An accounting system that acknowledges income and expenses as they are received and incurred. With this system, revenue is reported upon payment and expenses when cash is paid out.

Certificate of authority
A form that certifies that an LLC is allowed to conduct business in a state other than the state in which it was formed.

Disregarded entity
A single-owner business entity disregarded by the IRS for purposes of federal income tax. The owner of the LLC pays the business's portion of taxes along with their personal taxes.

Domestic LLC
An LLC that operates within the state in which it was formed.

Double taxation
The process by which a corporation pays taxes on its earnings, and the owners of the corporation—called shareholders—pay personal income taxes on profits they receive from the business.

Employer identification number (EIN)
A nine-digit number assigned to a business by the IRS for the purposes of filing and reporting taxes. An EIN is often referred to as a Social Security number for a business.

Entity classification regulations
Rules established by the IRS that enable the member(s) of an LLC to choose the manner in which they want their LLC to be taxed.

Fictitious business name
A name used by a business that is a name other than its registered name.

Foreign LLC
An LLC that conducts business in a state other than the state in which it was formed.

Franchise tax
A tax imposed on certain businesses for their operations within certain states.

General partnership
A business of two or more people that operates without having registered as a business entity.

Home occupation permit
A permit that allows you to establish and run a business from your home.

Initial report
A report filed with the state within a specified time after an LLC is formed. Initial reports are not required by every state.

Judicial dissolution
A legal process within which a court terminates a business due to an event such as fraud or mismanagement.

Known claims
Claims by creditors of which members of an LLC are aware.

Limited partnership
A business entity with at least one general partner and one limited partner that is registered in a state.

Local business operating license
A license from your local or city government granting permission to operate a business.

Low-profit LLC
A for-profit organization that's structured like an LLC, but also required to provide a product or service that benefits the public.

Malpractice
Negligence or a mistake that causes harm to a client.

Mediation
An arrangement in which a third party works with the members of an LLC to attempt to resolve a dispute without having to take the matter to court.

Members
The owners of an LLC.

Mission statement
Part of a business plan that provides a brief explanation of the purpose of the business, often combining practical goals with a more idealized vision for the business.

Multi-member LLC
An LLC that has two or more members.

Operating agreement
A document that explains how an LLC will operate, based on the needs and wishes of its members. The agreement assures that everyone understands how the business will be run.

Partnership agreement
An agreement stating how a partnership will be run and outlining the rights and responsibilities of each partner.

Passive investors
Investors who are members of an LLC because of their financial contributions, but who do not have any say in how the business is managed.

Pass-through taxation
A tax system that enables the profits of a single-member LLC to be passed through to the owner's individual tax return and taxed at the individual rate.

Piercing the corporate veil
When a court ignores the limited liability of an LLC and holds its officers, directors, and members personally liable for its debts.

Professional liability insurance
A form of insurance, often called malpractice insurance, that protects members of professional LLCs from acts that are harmful to a client.

Professional LLC
A specialized type of LLC for licensed professionals such as lawyers, doctors, accountants, engineers, veterinarians, psychologists, or architects.

Provisions
The parts of an operating agreement, each of which contains specific types of information.

Recourse debt
Business debt that one member of a partnership has personally guaranteed.

Registered agent
A person or business authorized to receive legal correspondence on behalf of your LLC.

Responsible party
The person who applies for an employer identification number (EIN) for an LLC. The responsible party must be the person who owns or controls the business.

S-corporation
Also known as an S-corp, referring to a corporation that has been granted special tax status by the IRS. An S-corp is not a type of business entity, it's simply a corporation with a particular tax status.

Series LLC
A special type of LLC consisting of an umbrella, or parent entity, with one or more sub-LLCs, each of which operates as a separate business.

Single-member LLC
An LLC that has only one member.

Sole proprietor
Someone who owns and runs a business that has not been registered with the state.

Statement of purpose
Part of your LLC's Articles of Organization and required by some states, a statement of purpose lays out information regarding the business purpose of your LLC.

Statutory conversion
A method of changing a business from one type of business entity to another.

Tax matters partner
A member of an LLC who serves as a spokesperson for the business in any dealings with the IRS.

Tax termination
The termination of an LLC that is taxed under the default partnership method of taxation. A tax termination is triggered by the LLC transferring at least half its membership within a twelve-month time period.

Triggering event
An event or happening that requires a business to cease its operations and prepare for termination.

Unknown claims
Claims by creditors of which members of an LLC are unaware.

Voluntary dissolution
The voluntary termination of an LLC, as voted by its members.

Index

WHAT DID YOU THINK?

We rely on reviews and reader feedback to help our authors reach more people, improve our books, and grow our business. We would really appreciate it if you took the time to help us out by providing feedback on your recent purchase.

It's really easy, it only takes a second, and it's a tremendous help!

NOT SURE WHAT TO SHARE?

Here are some ideas to get your review started...

- *What did you learn?*
- *Have you been able to put anything you learned into action?*
- *Would you recommend the book to other readers?*
- *Is the author clear and easy to understand?*

TWO WAYS TO LEAVE AN AMAZON REVIEW

Use the camera app on your mobile phone to scan the QR code or visit the link below to record your testimonial and get your free book.

SCAN ME   or   www.quickstartguides.review/llc   **VISIT URL**

GET YOUR NEXT
QuickStart Guide®
FOR FREE

Leave us a quick video testimonial on our website and we will give you a **FREE *QuickStart Guide*** of your choice!

RECORD TESTIMONIAL   **SUBMIT TO OUR WEBSITE**   **GET A FREE BOOK**

TWO WAYS TO LEAVE A VIDEO TESTIMONIAL

Use the camera app on your mobile phone to scan the QR code or visit the link below to record your testimonial and get your free book.

or go.quickstartguides.com/free-qsg

 SCAN ME   **VISIT URL**

SAVE 10% ON YOUR NEXT
QuickStart Guide®

USE CODE: QSG10

www.quickstartguides.shop/business

www.quickstartguides.shop/rungrow

www.quickstartguides.shop/dmarketing

www.quickstartguides.shop/accounting

Use the camera app on your mobile phone to scan the QR code or visit the link below the cover to shop.
Get 10% off your entire order when you use code 'QSG10' at checkout at www.quickstartguides.com

CLYDEBANK MEDIA

QuickStart Guides®

PROUDLY SUPPORT ONE TREE PLANTED

One Tree Planted is a 501(c)(3) nonprofit organization focused on global reforestation, with millions of trees planted every year. ClydeBank Media is proud to support One Tree Planted as a reforestation partner.

Every dollar donated plants one tree and every tree makes a difference!

Learn more at www.clydebankmedia.com/charitable-giving or make a contribution at onetreeplanted.org.

Made in the USA
Coppell, TX
09 November 2024

39926275R00103